LATERAL
LOGICIAN

LATERAL
LOGICIAN

300 MIND-STRETCHING PUZZLES

by
Edward J. Harshman,
Paul Sloane & Des Machale

Main Street
A division of Sterling Publishing Co., Inc.
New York

2 4 6 8 10 9 7 5 3 1

Published by Sterling Publishing Co., Inc.
387 Park Avenue South, New York, NY 10016
This book is comprised of material from the following Sterling titles:
Clever Lateral Thinking Puzzles © 1997 by Edward J. Harshman
Super Lateral Thinking Puzzles © 2000 by Paul Sloane and Des Machale
Tricky Lateral Thinking Puzzles © 1999 by Paul Sloane and Des Machale

© 2004 by Sterling Publishing Co., Inc
Distributed in Canada by Sterling Publishing
c/o Canadian Manda Group, One Atlantic Avenue, Suite 105
Toronto, Ontario, Canada M6K 3E7
Distributed in Great Britain by Chrysalis Books Group PLC
The Chrysalis Building, Bramley Road, London W10 6SP, England
Distributed in Australia by Capricorn Link (Australia) Pty. Ltd.
P.O. Box 704, Windsor, NSW 2756, Australia

Designed by StarGraphics Studio

Sterling 1-4027-1684-2

TABLE OF CONTENTS

INSTRUCTIONS

The puzzles in this book are all of a type known as lateral thinking puzzles, or situation puzzles. They should be fun—but they also help to develop skills in questioning, deduction, logic, and lateral thinking. They are based on a statement of a situation that you have to use as a starting point in order to arrive at a particular explanation or solution. Often there can be many possible scenarios that explain the puzzle, but you have to find the "right" answer.

It is better to do these puzzles in a small group rather than trying to solve them individually. Typically they contain insufficient information for you to immediately deduce the solution. You need to ask questions in order to gather more information before you can formulate solutions.

One person acts as quizmaster. He or she reads the puzzle aloud and reads the solution silently. The others ask questions in order to gather information, check assumptions, and test possible solutions. The quizmaster can answer in one of four ways: "Yes," "No," "Irrelevant," or "Please rephrase the question."

If people get stuck, the quizmaster can offer one or more of the clues given in the Clues section. The aim is to arrive at the solution given in the Answers section, not simply to find a situation that satisfies the initial conditions.

As with most problems we face, it is best to start by testing your assumptions, and by asking broad questions that establish general conditions, motives, and actions. Don't narrow in on specific solutions until you have first established the broad parameters of what is going on.

When you get stuck, attack the problem from a new direction—think laterally!

PUZZLES

BATTY
BANDITRY

Welcome, Slasher

Bob, a fifteen-year-old boy with a record of violent crimes, approached a screened porch. Taking out a switchblade, he cut through every screen panel with large diagonal rips. A police officer drove by in a patrol car, saw what the boy was doing, and was pleased. Explain.

Clues: 128 /Answer: 206

SMASHED TAILLIGHTS

Later, Bob picked up a tire wrench and smashed the tail-lights of a car that he had never seen before. Police officers witnessed his act and arrested not him, but the owner of the car. Explain.

Clues: 128 / Answer: 206

SUPPOSED TO KILL?

A man drew a gun, pointed it at another man who was known to be totally law-abiding, and pulled the trigger. Click! The gun wasn't loaded. Everyone present, which included at least ten people, was surprised and outraged. Why was the intended victim blamed for the incident?

Clues: 128 / Answer: 207

BURNING DOWN THE BUILDING

An old apartment building caught fire. Most apartments were damaged badly, and many people were left homeless. An investigator arrived from the fire department. A shady man pulled him aside into a dark corner of the building and handed him five hundred-dollar bills. "It would be better for both of us," said the shady man, "if something went wrong with the investigation. Lose the papers, or whatever." The investigator looked at the money and protested, "But the landlord will want to file an insurance claim and need our report." "He won't mind," the shady man replied. "Be nice to the other fire victims and don't ask questions." The investigator pocketed the money and conveniently forgot the case. Why did the landlord not get upset?

Clues: 129 / Answer: 207

CAUGHT IN THE ACT

A woman walked into a police station. "I want to report a pickpocket," she announced. A man staggered in behind her, his hand in her coat pocket. "Arrest that man!" she continued, pointing to him. He was arrested, tried, and convicted of picking pockets. Why did he enter the police station in a posture that obviously suggested his crime?

Clues: 129 / Answer: 207

SLIPPERY SIDNEY SLIPPED UP

Slippery Sidney rented a car for a month. He returned it and paid the rental fee. Three months later, he was arrested for attempting to defraud the rental-car company. What happened?

Clues: 129 / Answer: 207

HONEST IVAN

The rental-car company, after convicting Sidney, advised all personnel to watch for odometer tampering. Later, Ivan rented a car in central Florida. Two days later, it was badly damaged when a truck lost control and hit it on a thruway in Virginia. The odometer reading was too low to account for the trip from Florida to Virginia, but Ivan easily went free. How?

Clues: 130 / Answer: 208

ROBBING THE BANK

Upon being tipped off that a large organization paid its employees on a certain day, and that its employees went to a specific bank to cash their paychecks at a certain time on that day, a gang decided to rob the bank at exactly that day and time. They would have been better off if they had robbed the bank on any other day than that one or at any other time during that day. Why?

Clues: 130 / Answer: 208

HE CALLED THE POLICE

A burglar broke into a house, intending to steal from it. While still in the house, he called the police. Why?

Clues: 130 / Answer: 208

ARRESTED ANYWAY

Rocky Redneck carried a gun. He had a state-issued firearm permit that allowed him to do so, and he was careful to obey the law. One day, he went to visit his relatives across the country, in another state. Rocky had a firearm permit from that state, too; and he could legally carry his gun there. He found out from the airlines that he could take his gun with him if it was declared to the airline staff and was in checked baggage. Ever the law-abiding citizen, Rocky packed the gun in a suitcase, told the airline clerk about it, and had the suitcase checked. So why was Rocky arrested for weapons possession?

Clues: 131 / Answer: 208

No Ransom Demand

A man entered a government building and went through a weapons-detector search. Then he entered a government office and displayed a sawed-off shotgun. "Up against the wall, everyone!" he ordered. Then, after everyone complied, he called the police. When police officers arrived, he put down his gun and cooperated with them. He refused to defend himself in court and was convicted of assault with a deadly weapon and given a long prison sentence. "What's the point of taking people hostage if you don't make a ransom demand?" asked a news reporter. "I thought of making one," he replied, "but there just didn't seem to be any point to it." So why did the man act as he did?

Clues: 131 / Answer: 209

ESCAPING THE KIDNAPPERS

Brenda had been kidnapped. She was locked in a room and placed on the floor, hands tied behind her back. She knew where she was, but had no chance of escape. Or did she? A telephone was on a table. She waited until no one was nearby, then she pulled the telephone to the floor. Alas! A dial lock! What did she do?

Clues: 131 / Answer: 209

PEOPLE PUZZLES

HEARING THEM QUICKLY

"Hey, Pop! Can I have some money?" asked Dana. "The Electric Earsplitters are giving a concert here in town next week, and I really want to hear it." His father put down the television listings, turned off the TV, and firmly declined. "But that's my favorite group!" protested Dana. "I want to buy tickets real fast so I can hear them perform as soon as possible." "If that's what's most important to you," replied his father, "then you won't need any tickets." Explain.

Clues: 132 / Answer: 209

MOTORCYCLE MADNESS

Together, Peter and his brother Jamie owned some land in the country. They enjoyed outdoor activities on it, but lately had had trouble with motorcyclists who ignored the fences and no-trespassing signs and noisily rode where they wished. One day, Jamie and his wife Amy were outside, peacefully eating a picnic lunch, when two people on a motorcycle cut through the grass and raced past them. Jamie jumped up and ran to his car to chase them, when Peter drove up in his jeep. "They went that way!" shouted Jamie, pointing. Peter gunned the motor in hot pursuit. "Did you catch them?" Amy asked them later. "No," replied Peter. "They slipped through a gap in the fence and escaped." Why was Amy pleased?

Clues: 132 / Answer: 210

A CRYING PROBLEM

Sandra had problems with her husband and was on strained terms with his parents. Nevertheless, one day she called them and chatted for about fifteen minutes. They thanked her for calling and told her that they felt better about her after talking. When she hung up the telephone, she burst into tears. Explain.

Clues: 132 / Answer: 210

SHE NEVER FIXED HIM UP

When Mitch started working in the small office, he was noted for his shyness. Anna, a co-worker, found out about his recent divorce and offered to set up a blind date for him. Eager to establish a new social life, he accepted her offer. But she never followed up on it, and he never met anyone else. Why did Mitch not mind?

Clues: 133 / Answer: 210

HAPPY THAT SHE CURSED HIM

A man called the woman he loved, and she cursed at him and hung up angrily. Why was he happy?

Clues: 133 /Answer: 210

EVICTED

A man locked his son out of the house. The son thanked him. Explain.

Clues: 133 /Answer: 210

CRAZY CARS AND TRICKY TRANSPORT

DRIVING THE WRONG CAR

Hermie the Hermit had a car that needed repair but was still drivable. He had another car that worked. He drove the first car to a repair shop. To avoid asking someone else to drive him home, he had fastened his two cars together and towed one with the other. He therefore arrived at the repair shop with two cars instead of one and could easily drive away with the working car. But why did he tow the working car with the broken one, and not the other way around?

Clues: 134 /Answer: 211

SAFE SMASH-UP

A car slowly started to move forward. Then it picked up speed. Faster and faster it went, until it crashed through a guardrail and went over a cliff. It fell over a hundred feet and was badly damaged. No one was killed or injured. In fact, no one was even afraid of being killed or injured. Why not?

Clues: 134 /Answer: 211

CONTAGIOUS CARSICKNESS?

Stan and Jan were driving along a highway. Fran, a small child strapped into the backseat, said "I feel sick." "It's probably carsickness," replied Jan. "We'll be stopping soon," said Stan, "then you can get out for some fresh air." Less than ten minutes later, Stan shut off the engine and they all got out of the car. But within half an hour, Jan complained: "Fran has motion sickness, and I do, too." Jan did not normally get carsick. What was happening?

Clues: 134 /Answer: 211

WHAT DRAINED THE BATTERY?

Walter forgot to allow for the slowness of traffic in the rain and was late for work. He hurriedly drove into the parking lot, parked, turned off the windshield wipers, jumped out of his car, slammed the door, and ran for the main entrance. That evening, he could not get the car started. The battery was dead. He got a jump start from a co-worker, drove home, and used his battery recharger to put a good charge on the battery. But despite careful testing, he never found out why the battery went dead. Can you?

Clues: 135 /Answer: 211

SEASONAL MILEAGE

Claude gets noticeably better mileage while driving the last mile to or from work than he does during any other part of the trip in summer. But not in winter. Why not?

Clues: 135 /Answer: 211

SHE ARRIVED ON TIME

Daryl and Carol had arranged to meet at a coffeehouse but something came up. Daryl looked in the phone book, found Carol's home phone number and called her. "I know we were supposed to meet in the coffeehouse in two hours, but my boss called and I have to reschedule. I'm due at the office two hours from now." "That's too bad," replied Carol, "but I can meet you at the coffeehouse in two minutes if you'd like." Daryl agreed and, because he lived right across the street from it, was there in two minutes. He was content to wait. but Carol was waiting for him. "You live clear across town," noted Daryl. "How could you get here so fast?"

Clues: 136 /Answer: 212

A Token Wait in a Token Line

Smart Stephanie worked in a city and took the subway to work every morning during rush hour. In the evening, also during rush hour, she took the subway home again. To use the subway, she had to put a subway token into a turnstile as she entered the station from the street. Although she was one of numerous commuters at those hours and had to stand in crowded subway cars, she never had to wait in a long line to buy tokens. Why not?

Clues: 136 /Answer: 212

The Late Train

Amanda got onto a train. After traveling about one thousand miles, she got off. She arrived at her destination forty-five minutes late. There had been no delays, and the train had picked her up on time. Why was it late?

Clues: 136 /Answer: 212

ODD OFFICES

Stubborn Steve

Steve went to an office supply store and got a ream (500 sheets) of standard-size paper. "We have a special today," a sales clerk told Steve helpfully as he carried the ream to the checkout counter. "It's a better grade of paper than what you're carrying, and it's cheaper, too." Steve investigated and he discovered that the paper on sale was the same size, same color, and of a heavier weight than the paper he had in his hand. Used in certain printers or copiers, it would be less likely to jam than would the paper Steve had chosen. And sure enough, it was much less expensive. Why, therefore, did Steve decline the paper on sale and retain his original choice?

Clues: 137 /Answer: 212

MAKING THE GRADE

Nervous Nell, a college student with a straight-A average, went into her professor's office. She told the receptionist she was worried about her grade on the final paper for her course. "I want to be sure I pass this course," said Nell. "Is there some way I can be notified of my final grade as soon as possible?" The receptionist, sympathetic to her concern, replied, "If you hand in a self-addressed stamped postcard with your term paper, the professor will write the grade for the paper and the course on it and mail it to you as soon as the paper is graded. That's much faster than waiting for a transcript." "Oh," said Nell, "but I don't think I can do that." Why not?

Clues: 137 /Answer: 212

Spaced-Out at the Computer

A secretary was working at her computer. She had a chart loaded into her word-processing program and had to rearrange it. The hard part of her job was removing extra spaces. The word-processing program had a "replace" command. She could replace any sequence of characters with any other sequence, or with nothing at all. So how could she replace many spaces in a row with only one space? This is not the same as replacing all spaces with nothing, because then there wouldn't be the one space that she wanted.

Clues: 137 / Answer: 213

The Fast Elevator Trip

Bill was nearly late for an appointment in a tall office building. He ran into the building, reached the elevators that led to the correct range of floors, pressed the button, and waited. After a tense few minutes, an elevator arrived and opened its doors to receive passengers. Why didn't he get on?

Clues: 138 / Answer: 213

The Nonstop Elevator Trip

Bill got to his appointment on time. "I was worried about those elevators for a minute," said Bill, "but I figured out a way to get here faster." Then he explained his reasoning. "Never thought of that," said Jill, who worked there and greeted him, "but if you just get in an elevator, it sure can take a long time. I have a way to beat the system, too." "What's your way?" he asked. "I just get in, and when the elevator first stops, I get out," she replied. He couldn't figure out how that strategy would save any time. Can you?

Clues: 138 / Answer: 213

TOO PRECISE

Mary and Jerry were working in an office. Jerry was writing something, and Mary looked over his shoulder. "That's too precise," complained Mary. "It should be more vague, harder to understand." "That's crazy!" replied Jerry. "The entire philosophy of the business we are in is based on that kind of reasoning I know, but that's not being tolerated here!" "Yes, precision is our great strength," admitted Mary, "and ordinarily I'd agree with you. But in this particular instance, no." Where were they?

Clues: 138 /Answer: 213

EXCEPTIONALLY VAGUE

Mary heard Jerry out, explaining what he was writing, and easily agreed that it should be deliberately misleading. What was he writing?

Clues: 139 /Answer: 214

THE HOSTILE VOTER

Charlie received a telephone call from the office of a local politician. A fast-talking campaign volunteer explained the benefits of the candidate, including a lecture on his platform. Charlie asked if the volunteer was calling at the request of the candidate, heard the volunteer's answer, and announced firmly that he intended to vote for the candidate's opponent. Then he hung up. Explain.

Clues: 139 /Answer: 214

A MYSTERY FAX

When his private phone line rang and he picked it up, the business executive heard a loud, squealing noise. Why did he receive a fax call on his private line, a phone that was known not to have a fax machine connected to it?

Clues: 139 /Answer: 214

ANOTHER MYSTERY FAX

One of the executive's subordinates sent a fax to a colleague. The subordinate would have preferred to have merely called the colleague in an ordinary way, but instead handwrote a note and faxed it. Why?

Clues: 140 /Answer: 214

PROBLEMS WITH PERSONNEL

Raymond, a business executive in a large company, needed a department head. After placing a classified ad, he reviewed the responses sent on to him from the personnel department. When a colleague mentioned a potentially suitable friend of hers who was looking for work, Raymond tracked him down, interviewed him, checked references, and hired him. Then he complained vigorously to the personnel department. Why?

Clues: 140 /Answer: 215

More Problems with Personnel

It's true that all the references checked out positively, and the interviewee was hired. But a few weeks later, the colleague who recommended him to Raymond showed up—and the newly hired department head was fired on the spot. Explain.

Clues: 140 /Answer: 215

Dismaying Dizziness

Raymond finally got an honest department head and had her office redecorated, installing new wallpaper, a refinished desk, and a bright ceiling lamp. He had received complaints that that office was dark and dirty, and he had no wish to alienate a new employee without cause. Unfortunately, she complained of dizziness in her office. He entered it to investigate, and he got dizzy too. Neither of them was dizzy anywhere else. What was the problem?

Clues: 141 /Answer: 215

ASININE ACTIONS

Giving Wayne the Boot

Wayne was asleep when a boot crashed through his bedroom window, waking him up. Loud music came from the house next door, further irritating him. He jumped up, shook his fist at his neighbor's house, and shouted some obscenities toward it. "It's three a.m.," he yelled truthfully. "If you don't turn down that racket now, I'm calling the cops!" The music persisted and Wayne did as he had threatened and called the police. When they arrived, the officers refused to prosecute for the noise, even though it was obviously excessively loud. After the police officers explained the facts to Wayne, he was happy to forgive not only the noise but also the broken window. Explain.

Clues: 141 /Answer: 215

RACING THE DRAWBRIDGE

Park Street included a drawbridge over a river. As its warning lights flashed, Clarence proceeded toward the bridge. The barriers were lowered, blocking the road. Clarence ignored them. The drawbridge itself opened, and Clarence gunned the motor and aimed right at it. But there was no collision. Why not?

Clues: 142 /Answer: 216

RECYCLED SALT

Can salt be recycled? How?

Clues: 142 /Answer: 216

SCARED OF HER SHADOW?

Wacky Wendy, who lives in Florida, finds it particularly important, when she is driving and sees the shadow of her car, to roll down her window. Why?

Clues: 142 /Answer: 216

PICTURE THE TOURISTS

"I have a manual focus camera," said Sherman Shutterbug to his friend Sal as they sat next to each other on a tour bus. "Mine is autofocus," replied Sal. "It's much quicker, because the camera measures the distance to whatever I'm photographing and focuses automatically." "Then I think we'd better change places," said Sherman. Why?

Clues: 143 /Answer: 216

The Mirror

A mirror is mounted over the headboard of a bed. It is there because someone has a bad back. Explain.

Clues: 143 /Answer: 216

The Empty Wrapper

A woman was at the checkout lane of a supermarket. She removed several items from her cart and put them on the conveyor belt that led to the cashier. The cashier noted their prices and passed the items along to be bagged. A perfectly ordinary process, but one of the items entered and passed along was an empty wrapper. The cashier realized that the wrapper was empty, but charged for it anyway. Why?

Clues: 143 /Answer: 217

SECRET FUEL

Marvin often sneaked into his neighbor's driveway in the middle of the night in the course of playing a prank. He would quietly unscrew the fuel cap from his neighbor's car and pour gasoline into its fuel tank. What was he up to?

Clues: 144 /Answer: 217

FORGOT TO STOP?

Angus was driving along a road at about thirty miles per hour. Suddenly, he jumped out of his car. He had not applied the brakes, and the car was still moving. He was not a stunt man for a movie or otherwise involved in deliberately risky activity. What happened?

Clues: 144 /Answer: 217

SHORT-LIVED MESSAGES

Yolanda regularly writes and destroys messages to herself. Usually, people write such notes as reminders, such as in calendars. But Yolanda never expects to forget what was in the messages. Why write them?

Clues: 145 /Answer: 217

MORE SHORT-LIVED WRITING

Yolanda often passes a writing instrument across a surface for which it is intended and, within a few seconds, erases the result. What is she doing?

Clues: 145 /Answer: 218

HAPHAZARD HAPPENINGS

THE MAIL IS IN!

One day earlier, little Oscar had mailed an order form for a wanted toy. Now, he was constantly pestering his mother to let him check the mail. Suddenly, looking out the window at the apartment complex mailboxes, he shouted, "The mail is in! The mail is in!" Neither he nor his mother had seen a mail carrier, mail truck, or any activity near the mailboxes, but Oscar was right, it was in. How had he known?

Clues: 145 / Answer: 218

MAGAZINE SUBSCRIPTIONS

Magazines often contain postcards meant for use by new subscribers. Some people consider them a nuisance and just toss them out. Some don't, even though they won't ever use them for their intended purpose. Why not throw them away?

Clues: 146 / Answer: 218

Soliciting in Seattle

Two friends, who lived in different well-to-do neighborhoods in Seattle, were conversing. "Almost every week, I get a few people who knock on my door and ask for money," said one. "Odd. That rarely happens to me," replied the other. But there is a good explanation for the difference. What is it?

Clues: 146 / Answer: 218

It's a Dog's Life

Fred and Jed saw a badly injured puppy. It had been hit by a car, and its left eye and part of its left front leg were missing. Fortunately, it had received competent treatment. A bandage covered what remained of its left front leg, and a patch was fastened over the left half of its face. Fred picked up the puppy and stroked it gently. It whimpered weakly as he put it down. "Poor thing," said Jed. "Look what it's been through." Fred nodded his head grimly. "I know. But it will almost certainly be alive in a year. That healthy-looking dog over there won't," he added, pointing to a frisky dog that wagged its tail eagerly. What was Fred's reasoning?

Clues: 147 / Answer: 219

Not from the USA

Belinda Blabbermouth told a riddle. "I am standing in a place where I can travel north, south, east, or west, and soon be in the USA. Where am I?" After everyone gave up, she laughed, "The USA, of course!" After a few seconds, someone else spoke up: "Not necessarily. The country I come from, for example." Where was he from?

Clues: 147 / Answer: 219

DOTS ON THE I'S

"The teacher marked you wro-ong," Jimmy sang out teasingly during school recess. "You didn't put dots on all your I's!" "Is that so!" countered Timmy. "Betcha don't know how to draw a small I with a dot on it!" he challenged. Jimmy did so, and Timmy looked defeated. A few moments later, Timmy retorted, "Well, now I have dots over my I's and you don't!" One glance at Timmy and Jimmy burst out laughing. So did Timmy. Half the class did, too. Explain.

Clues: 147 /Answer: 219

POWER FAILURE

While Horace slept peacefully, a transformer on the street burned out and stopped all electrical power to his house. The power was restored two hours later, while Horace was still asleep. He awoke the next morning and noted with annoyance that all of his digital clocks were blinking and needed to be reset. "I hate power failures," he grumbled, as he carried his battery-powered watch to the VCR, the microwave oven, and other devices that needed to have their clocks reset. But Horace had no idea that the power had failed during the night, much less how long. Explain.

Clues: 148 /Answer: 219

AFRAID OF THE COUNTRY

"The city is so hot and sticky during the summer," Willie said to his friend Nicolai. "I've got a house in the country. Can you join me there next weekend?" Nicolai smiled. "Ah, the country. Like a farm?" "Yes, you could say that," continued Willie. "It used to be a farm a long time ago." "That's good," continued Nicolai. "When I was a boy in Russia, I lived on a farm. There were cows and pigs, and they were like my friends. It will be good to go away from this hot city and be on a farm again." "You'll like it. It's so peaceful there," said Willie, continuing. "Nice and quiet. No cars. Not even animals." Nicolai suddenly stiffened, and stared straight ahead hardly breathing for close to a minute. "No," he eventually whispered quietly, "I cannot. Thank you for your lovely offer. I would like to, but cannot go." Why was Nicolai terrified at the thought of Willie's country house?

Clues: 148 /Answer: 219

LONG-LIFE BULBS

Eccentric Eric flipped an ordinary light switch in his living room. The lights went on, apparently in an ordinary way. But there was special hidden circuitry involved. He was right when he boasted, "My lights are wired so that the bulbs last much longer than average. I rarely have to change them." Explain.

Clues: 148 /Answer: 220

THEY HAD A BALL

Two men stood on a softball field and practiced throwing and catching just before a game. "Over here! Over here!" shouted Ned, slapping his fist into his mitt. Ted threw the softball to him. "Good catch! Throw me a grounder!" shouted Ted. Ned returned the ball by throwing it along the ground, as requested. "Now a high one! Right here! Right here!" Ted threw the ball high in the air—and Ned ran about ten feet to his left, reached up, and caught the ball easily. "Good arm, but your aim is a little crooked," he announced. "No it isn't," replied Ted." "So what's wrong with throwing the high ball right to where I was standing?" retorted Ned. What indeed?

Clues: 149 /Answer: 220

who didn't really care as long as the payment had arrived. "But although I wrote the other one first and mailed it first, I'm not surprised that it arrived later." Why?

Clues: 150 / Answer: 221

I'VE GOT YOUR NUMBER

Kingfist, a bookie well known for aggressive collection practices, was pursuing Sam Skiptown, who owed him money. From a distance, he spotted Sam and quietly followed him to his house. The house was well guarded, with a burglar alarm system and a climbable but inconvenient fence. Kingfist made plans. Within a week, he called Sam and warned him: "Pay now, or take the consequences." Sam was horrified. "How did you get my number?" he asked. "No questions," ordered Kingfist. "Let's just say I went to a lot of trouble to ask you nicely." Sam never figured out how Kingfist learned his telephone number, which was unpublished and known to only a few trusted friends. Can you?

Clues: 150 / Answer: 221

COLLECTING BACKWARDS

Kingfist forced a debtor to write him a check. Then he took it to the bank to cash it. Why did he first deposit money in the debtor's account?

Clues: 150 / Answer: 221

BETTER LATE THAN PROMPT

Kingfist was engaging in his usual habit of bullying a debtor into paying. "You don't have the cash? I'll tell you what I'm going to do," explained Kingfist. "Sign this contract, and I'll tear up this one you signed earlier." The debtor reviewed the contracts and saw that the old one was his original loan and

BALLPARK BEFUDDLEMENT

Nine men stood together at the edge of a field. One of them watched a ball intently and swung at it. Missed! He took another swing. Whack! The ball sailed up and to the left. A third swing. Zoom! This ball soared up and directly forward, and the man was pleased. Why didn't anyone run to retrieve the third ball?

Clues: 149 /Answer: 220

CRASS CREDITORS AND DULL DEBTORS

OVERDUE PAYMENT

Jim sent a payment on a debt every month. One month, he accidentally missed the deadline and got a warning. He was eager to pay as quickly as possible and feared that a mailed check might be delayed in the mail, but didn't want to pay extra for registered mail, overnight delivery, or anything else. How did he minimize the chance of a delayed payment?

Clues: 149 /Answer: 220

WRONG ORDER

Jim waited. Sure enough, he got a message that the pay-ment had arrived as he expected. Then he got a telephone call from his creditor, who had a secretary with an unusu-al attention to detail. "You sent next month's payment too," said the secretary. "I figured that the check with the higher number would be for next month, and the one with the lower number was for this month. But the higher number check got here first." "It's up to you," replied Jim

the new one was for the same amount, but for smaller payments that added up to the same total as the old one. The new one, overall, meant that the debtor didn't have to come up with money as fast and actually had a lower interest rate. And the new contract had no penalties for late payment, including harassment rights, that were not in the old contract either. The debtor was happy to sign. "Thanks!" replied Kingfist. "I'll be seeing you!" And that's exactly what happened. Kingfist was delighted, and the debtor soon realized he had blundered by signing the new contract. Explain.

Clues: 151 /Answer: 221

THE DEBTOR PAID

Kingfist had trouble with another debtor. "What can you do about it?" was the debtor's attitude. "The collection hassle is more than the bad debt is worth, and we both know it." But within two months, the customer paid the loan in full. Why?

Clues: 151 /Answer: 222

DAFFY DOCTORING

SHE WAS IN THE HOSPITAL

Alan called the office where his wife worked. "I'm sorry," came the reply. "There was a bad accident on the highway a few minutes ago, and she's expected to be in the operating room for at least six hours." "That's too bad," he replied. "Can you ask her to call me when she gets out?" Sure enough, about six hours later, Alan heard from his wife. Why was she not upset that Alan didn't visit her personally?

Clues: 151 / Answer: 222

APPENDICITIS

Zeke and his wife lived in a rural area. One evening, his wife felt ill. Zeke called the local physician. "Doc, I think my wife may have appendicitis," he explained. "Nonsense! I took out her appendix myself five years ago," said the doctor. But Zeke's wife proved to have appendicitis. Explain.

Clues: 152 / Answer: 222

CROSSED VISION

If your eyes are crossed, then you see worse than usual. But if your fingers are crossed, then you may be able to see better than usual. Explain.

Clues: 152 / Answer: 222

NIGHT BLINDNESS CURE

What two questions can cure some cases of night blindness, without formal eye examinations or blood tests?

Clues: 153 / Answer: 223

A Sweet Problem

White, refined sugar is frowned on as a dietary supplement and is especially to be avoided by diabetics (other than as an emergency treatment for insulin overdose or similar problems) — except for what?

Clues: 153 /Answer: 223

Miracle Cures

Some resorts and shrines are known throughout the world for providing effective treatments for conditions believed to be incurable. One explanation is divine intervention, a literal miracle. Another is faith and belief in the cure. A third is an unknown but potentially discoverable scientific explanation, such as an unidentified ingredient in springwater. What is a fourth?

Clues: 153 /Answer: 223

Not a Trusted Doctor

Cassandra and her boyfriend went to a lecture. At it, a doctor described a reputed cure for senility. "Nonsense!" said Cassandra. "He is no more a doctor than I am." "What do you mean?" asked her boyfriend. "He showed us his medical school diploma." What did she mean?

Clues: 153 /Answer: 223

The Plumber's Pressure

A plumber received a checkup in the doctor's office. "You have high blood pressure," said the doctor, after measuring it with a cuff. "You'll have to watch the salt and take blood-pressure medication." "That makes no sense, Doc," replied the plumber. "Didn't you tell me last visit that I had something else the matter with me?" "Yes, I did," replied the doctor, "and you still do." "That's why I don't trust that pressure gauge of yours," said the plumber. Why was he skeptical?

Clues: 154 /Answer: 223

Rx Lead Poisoning

A doctor examined a new patient and identified the woman's ailment. Later, as they spoke, he filled in her records, including medical insurance coverage. Suddenly, the doctor said, "In that case, I would suggest you go to an old building and eat some lead paint chips from its walls." Why?

Clues: 154 /Answer: 224

Long Walk for the Disabled

A man had a serious accident and partially recovered from it. Previously, he was in good physical shape. Now, he was disabled, but not in a way that qualified him for handicapped parking rights. Instead, he often had to park farther from destinations than he did before the accident. Explain.

Clues: 154 /Answer: 224

ECCENTRIC ELECTRONICS

Happy with the TV Ad

A man went to a television station and bought one minute's worth of advertising time. He handed a videocassette to the station manager and learned to the second exactly when his one-minute tape would be on the station. Just before the scheduled time, the man turned on his TV set, tuned it to the correct channel, and waited. At exactly the time for his ad, a test pattern came on. The sound, an intense pure tone, did not change for a full minute. The picture stayed the same, too. Then the man, pleased, turned off his TV set. Explain.

Clues: 155 /Answer: 225

TIME FOR REPAIRS

Dilton got a new digital watch and put it on his wrist. At work, he looked at the office clock and checked his watch. They showed the same time. Later that morning, he couldn't make sense of what his watch showed and decided to return to the store with it. But before lunchtime, he again noted that his watch showed the correct time. During his lunch break, he returned to the store. But the salesclerk to whom he showed the watch noted that it showed the correct time, and Dilton agreed that it did. Dilton was soon satisfied that he had a watch that worked perfectly. But the clerk neither opened it for repairs nor replaced it. Explain.

Clues: 155 /Answer: 225

Strange Sounds

Modern movies, unlike those of half a century ago, are often made with picture and sound recorded at different times. Sound-effects technicians watch the picture and make the appropriate sounds, perhaps walking in place on a hard floor to generate the sound of footsteps. How can this method of recording sound be detected in the final movies?

Clues: 155 / Answer: 225

Watching the Game

Elmer had a sports bar, one with several TV screens hooked up to a satellite receiver and tuned to receive popular sports events. One day, there was a ball game in a stadium nearby. The game was blacked out from the local television stations and even from local satellite receivers, but Elmer and his customers saw the game on television anyway. How?

Clues: 156 / Answer: 225

DIGITAL DOWNFALL

Why do hi-fi enthusiasts sometimes dislike compact disks and other digital recording media?

Clues: 156 /Answer: 226

THE TV OBEYED

Jake had some friends over to watch a popular new movie on his brand-new big-screen TV with state-of-the-art surround-sound speakers. As the credits ended and everyone started to the kitchen for snacks, an obnoxious commercial came on. Jake turned to the set. "Oh, shut up!" he shouted angrily at the TV—and it did! Explain.

Clues: 156 /Answer: 226

THE VCR TIMERS

Benny and Jenny were busy hooking up a new videocassette recorder. "I'll never understand these instructions!" shouted Benny, as he tried to set the VCR timer to record his favorite show every other night. "They make no sense to me, either," admitted Jenny. They returned to the store for advice and the salesclerk admitted that the instructions confused him too. "I recommend this for most of my customers," he said, showing them a battery-powered device that looked like a VCR remote control unit. "You can set it to signal start-recording and stop-recording for any time you want, once a week, every day, or whenever." Benny and Jenny looked through its instruction book and understood it easily. "Great!" said Benny. "Now I can tape my favorite show every other night." "No you can't," admitted the salesclerk. "It won't let you do that—just every night or once a week." "Yes we can," replied Jenny. "After a trip to the hardware store, that is." How?

Clues: 157 /Answer: 226

The VCR Remote Control

After Benny and Jenny set up their VCR to record their show on alternate nights, Benny looked for the remote control to the other VCR in the bedroom. "I put it away so the dog wouldn't get it," explained Jenny. "That's a nuisance," replied Benny. "Then we can't operate the VCR while lying in bed." "Yes we can," replied Jenny. How?

Clues: 157 /Answer: 227

No Television Trouble

Stuart was driving a car along a highway. A small television set sat on the dashboard, and Stuart could see its screen. The theme music from Stuart's favorite television show came on. At a police roadblock set up to screen and catch lawbreakers, a state trooper observed Stuart and his television set, but did not warn or arrest him. Why not?

Clues: 158 /Answer: 227

Inefficiency Pays Off

A certain mechanical object is often made in several models by each of its manufacturers. Government regulations require that its retail sellers offer information that will allow part of the cost of operation to be calculated. Of a manufacturer, the models of the object offered can be ranked from least to most expensive. The cheapest model costs relatively little to buy and to operate and has simple controls. The most expensive model costs most to operate and generally has the most elaborate controls. But the most expensive model is not necessarily the one that is most effective at doing what it is designed to do. What is the object?

Clues: 158 /Answer: 227

MAD MONEY

WORTH TWENTY DOLLARS

Nick had a series 1950 $20 bill. Instead of saying "Twenty dollars" at the bottom, it said "Will pay to the bearer on demand twenty dollars." He told his friend Dick, "If I can get twenty dollars' worth of gold or silver, then I may as well exchange this bill at the Federal Reserve office that issued it." Was he right?

Clues: 159 / Answer: 227

SLOW-WITTED CUSTOMERS

In northern Florida, fast-food chains often have a pricing policy that works only because many customers do not think carefully. What is it?

Clues: 159 / Answer: 228

BANKING ON THE BOYCOTT

On the principal street of a small town, a fast-food restaurant chain was planning to open. Local citizens, wary of litter and disruption, and eager to defend the livelihoods of their local diners, planned retaliation. At a town meeting, a woman urged strict enforcement of litter and parking-meter laws. A man stood up and suggested something more devious: that everyone go there and order something, but insist on a special order (no lettuce with the hamburger, etc.) so as to overwhelm the help. Another man, who happened to work at the town bank, approved of the action, but recommended that they all come to his place of business first. Why?

Clues: 159 / Answer: 228

OLD MONEY BUT GOOD MONEY

What two changes affected U.S. currency in 1968 that, if considered together, scare certain conservatives?

Clues: 160 / Answer: 228

SECRET BUSINESS

Two men were on the telephone, discussing a multi-million-dollar business deal. They used electronic scramblers, so that no one could easily listen in on their conversation. They also each had much more sophisticated scramblers, which were harder to obtain and which encoded conversations more securely than the scramblers that they used. Why did they use the less secure scramblers?

Clues: 160 / Answer: 229

GAS-STATION GLITCH

During a fuel shortage, George drove to a gas station and waited in line behind many other motorists. A man in the familiar gas-station uniform walked over and explained to him, "We have a ten-dollar limit. To save time, we are taking cash only and collecting payment in advance." George gave the man a ten-dollar bill. When he reached the front of the line and parked in front of a pump, he asked for his ten dollars' worth of gas. "The limit is five dollars," replied the attendant. What happened?

Clues: 160 / Answer: 229

MARKETING MUDDLE

What carelessly marketed name of a car may provoke concerns about auto safety?

Clues: 161 / Answer: 229

EASY MONEY

The television set had a retail value of $100. Butch worked at the wholesale warehouse and said that stores bought them for $60 each. The warehouse bought them in large lots for $45 apiece. He offered to sell you all you want for $30 each. If they cost $45, then how could he make a profit at $30?

Clues: 161 /Answer: 229

TOO MUCH MONEY

An investor was reading the description of a proposed investment. It was a limited partnership, so that the investor would have no control over the management of the investment. But there were safeguards in place so that if the person who managed the investment made a profit, then the investor would too. Suddenly, the investor discovered something that made him decide not to invest. "Too much money," he muttered to himself, throwing the description onto his desk. Too little money invested in a company can be a bad sign, for it may go bankrupt. But why would the investor be afraid of too much money?

Clues: 161 /Answer: 229

GOOFY GAMBLING

LOTTERY LOGIC

Many states run lotteries as a way to raise money. For every dollar received from lottery-ticket sales, perhaps half a dollar is paid out to winners. Therefore, the weighted-average value of the expected winnings of a one-dollar ticket is perhaps half a dollar. Therefore, although a lottery ticket may be a fun expense because it carries a chance to get rich, it is never a good investment from a financial-planning perspective. Right?

Clues: 162 /Answer: 230

YOUTHFUL GAMBLE

Some people gamble irrationally and are at risk of losing more money than they can afford to. Laws exist, therefore, to prohibit gambling except under special circumstances. It would seem especially important to keep young adults from gambling, for bad habits can be formed while young that cannot be easily corrected later. But certain young adults are allowed to gamble, in that they pay money and receive something of greater or lesser value, in exchange for that money, that is partially determined by chance. Explain.

Clues: 162 /Answer: 230

STAGED ROULETTE

Police officers, their spouses, and their families put together a talent show to raise money for their retirement fund. One of the events at the show was a skit about the evils of gambling. In one scene, a misguided man lost most of his money to a crooked roulette-wheel operator. It was learned too late that the audience could see the stage from above and would observe the number into which a roulette ball would drop. What did the producers do?

Clues: 163 /Answer: 230

NORTH PUZZLES

THE DEADLY SCULPTURE

A penniless sculptor made a beautiful metal statue, which he sold. Because of this he died soon afterward. Why?

Clues: 163 / Answer: 231

PEAK PERFORMANCE

The body of a climber is found, many years after his death, a thousand feet below the summit of one of the world's highest mountains. In his pocket is a diary claiming that he had reached the summit and was on his way down. How was it discovered that he was not telling the truth?

Clues: 163 / Answer: 231

THE FATAL FISH

A man was preparing a fish to eat for a meal when he made a mistake. He then knew that he would shortly die. How?

Clues: 164 /Answer: 231

ADAM HAD NONE

Adam had none. Eve had two. Everyone nowadays has three. What are they?

Clues: 164 /Answer: 231

SHOT DEAD

A woman who was in a house saw a stranger walking down the road. She took a gun and shot him dead. The next day she did the same thing to another stranger. Other people saw her do it and knew that she had killed the two men, yet she was never arrested or charged. Why not?

Clues: 164 /Answer: 231

WOULD YOU BELIEVE IT?

Three people were holding identical blocks of wood. They released the blocks at the same time. The blocks of wood were not attached to anything. The first person's block fell downward. The second person's block rose up. The third person's block stayed where it was, unsupported. What was going on?

Clues: 164 /Answer: 231

JAILBREAK

A man planned his escape from prison very carefully. He could have carried it out in the dead of night but he preferred to do it in the middle of the morning. Why?

Clues: 164 /Answer: 231

SITTING DUCKS

Why does a woman with no interest in hunting buy a gun for shooting ducks?

Clues: 165 /Answer: 232

BALD FACTS

Mary, Queen of Scots was almost totally bald, and wore a wig to conceal this fact from her subjects. How was her secret revealed?

Clues: 165 /Answer: 232

Lethal Action

Brazilian authorities took actions to protect their fruit crops, and ten people from another continent died. How?

Clues: 165 /Answer: 232

Recognition

John lived in England all his life, until his parents died. He then went to Australia to visit relatives. His Aunt Mary had left England before he was born and had never returned. He had never met his Aunt Mary, had never spoken to her, and had never seen a picture of her. Yet he recognized her immediately in a crowded airport. How?

Clues: 165 /Answer: 232

Destruction

Commercial premises are destroyed by a customer. Afterward he disappears, but even if he had been caught he could not have been charged. Why?

Clues: 166 / Answer: 232

Wonderful Walk

A man and his dog went for a walk in the woods. When he returned home he invented something now worth millions of dollars. What was it?

Clues: 166 / Answer: 232

Pesky Escalator

A foreign visitor to London wanted to ride up the escalator at the subway station, but did not do so. Why?

Clues: 166 / Answer: 233

POLES APART

How did early explorers economize with provisions for a polar expedition?

Clues: 166 /Answer: 233

ARRESTED DEVELOPMENT

A bank robber grabbed several thousand dollars from a bank counter and, although he was armed, he was captured within a few seconds before he could leave the bank. How?

Clues: 166 /Answer: 233

HOLED OUT

A golfer dreamed all his life of getting a hole in one. However, when he eventually did get a hole in one, he was very unhappy and, in fact, quit golf altogether. Why?

Clues: 167 /Answer: 233

TRUNK-ATED

The police stop a car and they suspect that the trunk contains evidence linking the driver with a serious crime. However, they do not have a search warrant and if they open the trunk forcibly without probable cause, any evidence uncovered will not be admissible in court. How do they proceed?

Clues: 167 /Answer: 233

Sports Mad

Why was a keen sports fan rushing around his house looking for a roll of sticky tape?

Clues: 167 / Answer: 233

Appendectomy I & II

(There are two different solutions to this puzzle. Try both before looking at the answer to either.)

Why did a surgeon remove a perfectly healthy appendix?

Clues: 167 / Answers: 234

Riotous Assembly

After riots in a large institution, one section did not reopen for a long time after the other sections. Why?

Clues: 168 /Answer: 234

Kneed to Know

A woman places her hand on her husband's knee for an hour and then takes it off for ten minutes; then she places her hand on her husband's knee for another hour. Why?

Clues: 168 /Answer: 234

Bad Trip

An anti-drug agency distributed material to children in school. However, this had the opposite effect to what was intended. Why?

Clues: 168 /Answer: 234

WALLY TEST I

From the World Association of Learning, Laughter, and Youth (WALLY) comes the WALLY Test! It is a set of quick-fire questions. They may look easy, but be warned— they are designed to trick you. Write down your answers on a piece of paper and then see how many you got right. The time limit is three minutes.

1. When you see geese flying in a V formation, why is it that one leg of the V is always longer than the other?
2. Why are there so many Smiths in the telephone directory?
3. What is E.T. short for?
4. Where do you find a no-legged dog?
5. Approximately how many house bricks does it take to complete a brick house in England?
6. How do you stop a bull from charging?
7. What cheese is made backward?
8. Take away my first letter; I remain the same. Now take away my fourth letter; I remain the same. Now take away my last letter; I remain the same. What am I?
9. If a white man threw a black stone into the Red Sea, what would it become?
10. How do you make a bandstand?

Answers: 235

SOUTH PUZZLES

TWO LETTERS

Why did a man write the same two letters over and over again on a piece of paper?

Clues: 168 /Answer: 235

BODY OF EVIDENCE

A woman goes into a police station and destroys vital evidence relating to a serious crime, yet she walks away scot-free. How come?

Clues: 168 /Answer: 235

SHAKESPEARE'S BLUNDER

What major scientific blunder did Shakespeare include in his play Twelfth Night?

Clues: 169 /Answer: 235

NO CHARGE

A man guilty of a serious crime was arrested. The police had clear evidence against him, but he was set free without charge. Why?

Clues: 169 /Answer: 236

Pond Life

Why did the fashion for silk hats in the U.S. lead to a positive environmental increase in the number of small lakes and bogs?

Clues: 169 /Answer: 236

Shoe Shop Shuffle

In a small town there are four shoe shops of about the same size, each carrying more or less the same line in shoes. Yet one shop loses three times as many shoes to theft as each of the other shops. Why?

Clues: 169 /Answer: 236

CAESAR'S BLUNDER

Julius Caesar unexpectedly lost many of his ships when he invaded Britain. Why?

Clues: 170 / Answer: 236

SLOW DEATH

The ancient Greek playwright Aeschylus was killed by a tortoise. How?

Clues: 170 / Answer: 236

DRIVING AWAY

A man steals a very expensive car owned by a very rich woman. Although he was a very good driver, within a few minutes he was involved in a serious accident. Why?

Clues: 170 /Answer: 236

LIT TOO WELL?

Local government authorities in Sussex, England, installed many more lights than were needed. This resulted in considerable damage, but the authorities were pleased with the results. Why?

Clues: 170 /Answer: 237

QUICK ON THE DRAW

Every Saturday night, the national lottery is drawn with a multimillion-dollar first prize. A man sat down in front of his TV on Saturday night and saw that the numbers drawn exactly matched the numbers on his ticket for that day's lottery. He was thrilled but did not win a penny. Why not?

Clues: 171 / Answer: 237

SCALED DOWN

A butcher tried to deceive a customer by pressing down on the scale while weighing a turkey to make it appear heavier than it was. But the customer's subsequent order forced the butcher to admit his deception. How?

Clues: 171 / Answer: 237

THE HAPPY WOMAN

A woman going on a journey used a driver. Then she stopped and used a club to hit a large bird. She was very pleased. Why?

Clues: 171 /Answer: 237

VANDAL SCANDAL

The authorities in Athens were very concerned that tourists sometimes hacked pieces of marble from the columns of the ancient Parthenon buildings. The practice was illegal, but some people seemed determined to take away souvenirs. How did the authorities stop this vandalism?

Clues: 171 /Answer: 237

THE DEADLY DRAWING

A woman walked into a room and saw a new picture there. She immediately knew that someone had been killed. How?

Clues: 171 /Answer: 238

LEONARDO'S SECRET

Leonardo da Vinci created some secret designs for his paintings that he did not want anyone to see. He hid them, but they were recently discovered. How?

Clues: 172 /Answer: 238

DOWN PERISCOPE

A normal submarine was on the surface of the sea with its hatches open. It sailed due east for two miles. Then it stopped and went down 30 feet. It then sailed another half mile before going down a further 30 feet. All this time it kept its hatches fully open. The crew survived and were not alarmed in any way. What was going on?

Clues: 172 /Answer: 238

REALLY, CAPTAIN, THERE'S NOTHING TO WORRY ABOUT.

THE LETTER LEFT OUT

For mathematical reasons, in codes and ciphers it is desirable to have 25 (which is a perfect square) letters rather than the usual 26. Which letter of the English alphabet is left out and why?

Clues: 172 /Answer: 238

ARRESTED DEVELOPMENT—AGAIN

Two masked men robbed a bank, but they were very quickly picked up by the police. Why?

Clues: 172 /Answer: 238

TITANIC PROPORTIONS

How did the sinking of the Titanic lead directly to the sinking of another ship?

Clues: 172 /Answer: 238

THE MOVER

What can go from there to here by disappearing and then go from here to there by appearing?

Clues: 173 / Answer: 239

DEATH OF A PLAYER

A sportsman was rushed to a hospital from where he was playing and died shortly afterward. Why?

Clues: 173 / Answer: 239

Hot Picture

A woman paid an artist a large sum to create a picture, and she was very pleased with the results. Yet within a week, under her instructions, the picture was burned. Why?

Clues: 173 /Answer: 239

Genuine Article

A new play by Shakespeare is discovered. How did the literary experts prove it was authentic?

Clues: 173 /Answer: 239

Unhealthy Lifestyle

A man and a woman were exploring in the jungle. The woman had a very healthy lifestyle, while the man had a very unhealthy one. At the end of the exploration the woman died suddenly, but the man lived. Why?

Clues: 174 /Answer: 239

New World Record

A 102-year-old woman was infirm and inactive, yet one day she was congratulated on setting a new world record. What was it?

Clues: 174 /Answer: 239

EAST PUZZLES

Death by Romance

A newly married couple had a fireside supper together. They were so cozy and comfortable that they dozed off on the floor. Next morning they were both found dead where they lay. What had happened?

Clues: 174 /Answer: 240

Penalty

After a World Cup soccer match, two players swapped jerseys. The police immediately arrested them. Why?

Clues: 174 /Answer: 240

Golf Challenge I, II & III

(There are three different solutions to this puzzle. Try all three before looking at any of the answers.)

A man and a woman, who were both poor golfers, challenged each other to a match. The man scored 96 while the woman scored 98. However, the woman was declared the winner. Why?

Clues: 174 /Answers: 240

Poor Investment

A man bought a house for $1,000,000 as an investment. The house was well kept and carefully maintained by a good caretaker. Although the house remained in perfect structural order, within a few years it was worthless. Why?

Clues: 175 /Answer: 240

GIVE US A HAND . . .

A man searching for precious stones didn't find any, but found a severed human hand instead. What had happened?

Clues: 175 /Answer: 241

EVIL INTENT

A rich man meets a lady at the theater and invites her back to his house for a drink. She has a drink and then leaves. About an hour later he suddenly realizes that she intends to return and burgle his house. How does he know?

Clues: 175 /Answer: 241

TWO HEADS ARE BETTER THAN ONE!

Several Americans reported they saw a creature that had two heads, two arms, and four legs. They were surprised, frightened, and alarmed, and when they told their friends, nobody believed them. But they were reliable witnesses. What had they seen?

Clues: 175 /Answer: 241

Stone Me!

A boy flung a stone at a man and many people's lives were saved. How come?

Clues: 175 /Answer: 241

Judge for Yourself

The defendant in a major lawsuit asked his lawyer if he should send the judge a box of fine cigars in the hope of influencing him. The lawyer said it was a very bad idea and would prejudice the judge against him. The defendant listened carefully, sent the cigars, and won the case. What happened?

Clues: 176 /Answer: 241

LOVE LETTERS

Why did a woman send out 1,000 anonymous Valentine's cards to different men?

Clues: 176 / Answer: 241

STRANGE BEHAVIOR

A man was driving down the road into town with his family on a clear day. He saw a tree and immediately stopped the car and then reversed at high speed. Why?

Clues: 176 / Answer: 242

TREE TROUBLE

The authorities were concerned that a famous old tree was being damaged because so many tourists came up to it and touched it. So a wall was built around the tree to protect it. But this had the opposite effect of that intended. Why?

Clues: 176 / Answer: 242

THE BURIAL CHAMBER

Why did a man build a beautiful burial chamber, complete with sculptures and paintings, and then deliberately wreck it?

Clues: 176 / Answer: 242

MISCARRIAGE OF JUSTICE

An Italian judge released a guilty man and convicted an innocent man and as a result the confectionery industry has greatly benefited. Why?

Clues: 177 /Answer: 242

OFFENSES DOWN

The police in Sussex, England, found a new way to complete their form-filling and paperwork that significantly reduced crime. What was it?

Clues: 177 /Answer: 242

Police Chase

A high-speed police car chases a much slower vehicle in which criminals are escaping. But the police fail to catch them. Why?

Clues: 177 / Answer: 243

Café Society

A mall café is pestered by teenagers who come in, buy a single cup of coffee, and stay for hours, and thus cut down on available space for other customers. How does the owner get rid of them, quite legally?

Clues: 177 / Answer: 243

HI, JEAN!

A shop owner introduced expensive new procedures to make his premises more hygienic, but the results were the very opposite. Why?

Clues: 178 / Answer: 243

THE EMPTY MACHINE

A gumball machine dispensed gum when quarters were inserted. When the machine was opened, there was no money inside. A considerable number of gumballs had been consumed and the machine did not appear to have been interfered with in any way. What had happened?

Clues: 178 / Answer: 243

TAKE A FENCE

A man painted his garden fence green and then went on holiday. When he came back two weeks later, he was amazed to see that the fence was blue. Nobody had touched the fence. What had happened?

Clues: 178 / Answer: 243

WALLY TEST II

Time for another WALLY Test. The questions may look easy, but be warned—they're designed to trip you up. Write down your answers on a piece of paper and then see how many you got right. The time limit is three minutes.

1. What should you give an injured lemon?
2. If an atheist died in church, what would they put on his coffin?
3. Who went into the lion's den unarmed and came out alive?
4. A man rode down the street on a horse, yet walked. How come?
5. How can you eat an egg without breaking the shell?
6. Why was King Henry VIII buried in Westminster Abbey?
7. In China they hang many criminals, but they will not hang a man with a wooden leg. Why?
8. Why do storks stand on one leg?
9. A circular field is covered in thick snow. A black cow with white spots is in the middle. Two white cows with black spots are on the edge of the field. What time is it?
10. What was the problem with the wooden car with wooden wheels and a wooden engine?

Answers: 244

WEST
PUZZLES

SEX DISCRIMINATION

When lawyers went to prison to visit their clients they found that female lawyers were searched on entry but male lawyers were not. Why?

Clues: 178 /Answer: 244

WEIGHT LOSS

How did a Japanese diet clinic achieve great weight-loss results for its patients even though they did not change their diet or undertake more activity than normal?

Clues: 178 /Answer: 244

Psychic

You enter a parking lot and see a woman walking toward you. You then see a row of cars and know immediately which one is hers. How?

Clues: 179 /Answer: 244

The Happy Robber

A robber holds up a bank, but leaves with no money whatsoever. However, he is more pleased than if he had left with lots of money. Why?

Clues: 179 /Answer: 245

SIEGE MENTALITY

A city is under siege. The attackers have run out of ammunition and have suffered heavy casualties. Yet they take the city within a few days without further losses. How?

Clues: 179 / Answer: 245

CARRIER BAGS

During World War II, the British Royal Navy had very few aircraft carriers. What ingenious plan was devised to remedy this deficiency?

Clues: 179 / Answer: 245

THE CATHEDRAL UNTOUCHED

When London was bombed during World War II, St. Paul's Cathedral, in the center of the city, was never hit. Why not?

Clues: 180 / Answer: 245

BAGS AWAY

An airplane nearly crashed because one of the passengers had not fastened his suitcase securely enough. What happened?

Clues: 180 / Answer: 245

THE SAD SAMARITAN

Jim saw a stranded motorist on a country road. The motorist had run out of fuel, so Jim took him to the nearest garage and then drove him back to his car. Jim felt good that he had been such a good Samaritan, but discovered something later that made him very sad. What was it?

Clues: 180 /Answer: 246

THE TALLEST TREE

Men found what they suspected was the tallest tree in Australia. It was growing in the outback in rough terrain and with other trees around. They did not have any advanced instruments with them. How did they accurately measure the height of the tree?

Clues: 180 /Answer: 246

The Unwelcome Guest

A couple had a neighbor who continually arrived at mealtimes in the hope of getting a free meal. How did they use their very friendly dog to persuade the neighbor not to come for free meals again?

Clues: 180 /Answer: 246

Poor Show

Every time he performed in public, it was a complete flop. Yet he became famous for it, and won medals and prizes. People came from all over and paid to see him perform. Who was he?

Clues: 181 /Answer: 246

Message Received

How did Alexander the Great send secret messages with his envoy?

Clues: 181 /Answer: 246

The Mighty Stone

There was a huge boulder in the middle of a village green. It was too big to be moved, too hard to split, and dynamiting it was too dangerous. How did a simple peasant suggest getting rid of it?

Clues: 181 /Answer: 247

THE WORLD'S MOST EXPENSIVE CAR

The most expensive car ever made is for sale. Although many people want to own it and can afford to buy it, nobody will do so. Why?

Clues: 181 / Answer: 247

THE FATAL FALL

A woman dropped a piece of wood. She picked it up again and carried on as if nothing had happened. The wood was not damaged and she was not injured, but the incident cost her her life. Why?

Clues: 182 / Answer: 247

ELECTION SELECTION

There is an election in a deprived city area. All the political parties put up candidates, actively canvass, and spend money on their campaigns. Yet the election is won by a candidate who did not canvass or advertise and is unknown to all of the electors. How?

Clues: 182 / Answer: 247

WELL TRAINED

A man, a woman, and a child are watching a train come into a station. "Here it comes," says the man. "Here she comes," says the woman. "Here he comes," says the child. Who was correct?

Clues: 182 / Answer: 247

RAZOR ATTACK

A man had his throat attacked by a woman with a razor, yet he suffered no serious injuries. How come?

Clues: 182 / Answer: 248

THE OLD CROONER

How did Bing Crosby reduce the crime rate in various U.S. cities?

Clues: 183 / Answer: 248

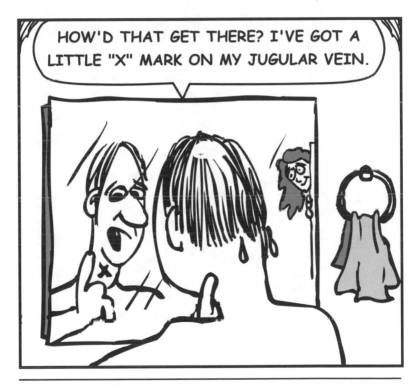

HOW'D THAT GET THERE? I'VE GOT A LITTLE "X" MARK ON MY JUGULAR VEIN.

THE PARSON'S PUP

Why did the vicar want only a black dog?

Clues: 183 / Answer: 248

Generosity?

A man took considerable trouble to acquire some money, but then quickly gave most of it away. Why?

Clues: 183 /Answer: 248

Watch That Man!

A runner was awarded a prize for winning a marathon. But the judges disqualified him when they saw a picture of his wristwatch. Why?

Clues: 183 /Answer: 248

TRICKY
PUZZLES

THE TRACKS OF MY TIRES

The police found a murder victim and they noticed a pair of tire tracks leading to and from the body. They followed the tracks to a nearby farmhouse where two men and a woman were sitting on the porch. There was no car at the farmhouse and none of the three could drive. The police arrested the woman. Why?

Clues: 183 / Answer: 249

THE UPSET WOMAN

When the woman saw him she was upset. Even though she had never seen him before, she had left some food for him because she knew he would be hungry. But he could not reach the food because he had an iron bar across his back. He died soon after and the woman was pleased. What's going on?

Clues: 184 / Answer: 249

BERTHA'S TRAVELS

Every day Bertha travels 30 miles in the course of her work. She doesn't travel in a wheeled vehicle and never has problems with traffic, the police, weather, or airports. What does she do?

Clues: 184 / Answer: 249

SICK LEAVE

Walter spent three days in the hospital. He was neither sick nor injured, but when it was time to leave he had to be carried out. Why?

Clues: 184 /Answer: 249

TOP AT LAST

William was the least intelligent and laziest boy in a class of 30 students who took an examination. Yet when the results were announced, William's name was at the top of the list. How come?

Clues: 184 /Answer: 249

CRIMINAL ASSISTANCE

The police put up notices warning the public about a certain type of crime, but this actually helped the criminals. How?

Clues: 184 /Answer: 249

IN THE MIDDLE OF THE NIGHT

A man wakes up at night in the pitch dark. He knows that on his bedside table are a razor, a watch, and a glass of water. How can he reach out onto the table and be sure to pick up the watch without touching either the razor or the glass of water?

Clues: 185 /Answer: 249

HONORABLE INTENT

Six people who do not know each other get together to honor a seventh person unknown to all of them. Why?

Clues: 185 /Answer: 250

SHELL SHOCK

Why do players very rarely win at the "shell game," where they have to say which of three shuffled shells covers a pea?

Clues: 185 /Answer: 250

WONDERFUL WEATHER

A ship sank in perfect weather conditions. If the weather had been worse, the ship would probably not have sunk. What happened?

Clues: 185 / Answer: 250

MATERIAL WITNESS

In the fabric shop, the curtains are neatly arranged by style. The floral-patterned ones are in a section marked "Floral," the plain ones are in a section marked "Plain," and the striped ones are in a section marked "Striped." But one pair with vertical blue stripes is not in the "Striped" section. Why not?

Clues: 185 / Answer: 250

DENISE AND HARRY

Denise died at sea while Harry died on land. People were pleased that Harry had died and even more pleased that Denise had died. Why?

Clues: 185 / Answer: 250

MECHANICAL ADVANTAGE

A driver had a problem with his car in a remote area miles from the nearest garage. He stopped at a little candy store, where his problem was quickly solved. How?

Clues: 186 / Answer: 250

LIFESAVER

A politician made a speech that saved his life even before he gave the speech. How?

Clues: 186 /Answer: 250

UNFINISHED BUSINESS

What work can a sculptor never finish?

Clues: 186 /Answer: 251

THE DEADLY DRESSER

A healthy man got dressed and then lay down and died. Why?

Clues: 186 /Answer: 251

LANDLUBBER

A man sailed single-handed around the world in a small boat. Yet he was always in sight of land. How come?

Clues: 186 /Answer: 251

ANOTHER LANDLUBBER

A man went around the world in a ship. Yet he was always in sight of land. How come?

Clues: 187 /Answer: 251

PLANE AND SIMPLE

A boy who is three feet tall puts a nail into a tree at his exact height. He returns two years later when he has grown by six inches and the tree has grown by twelve inches. How much taller is the nail than the boy?

Clues: 187 /Answer: 251

JERICHO

A man was building a house when it collapsed all around him. He wasn't injured or upset, and he calmly started to rebuild it. What was going on?

Clues: 187 /Answer: 251

SUPERIOR KNOWLEDGE

When the mother superior returned to the convent after a weekend away, she immediately noticed that a man had been there—and that was strictly against the rules. How did she know?

Clues: 187 / Answer: 251

HALF FOR ME AND HALF FOR YOU

It is said that Lucrezia Borgia once split an apple in half and shared it with a companion. Within 10 minutes her companion was dead and Lucrezia survived. How come?

Clues: 187 / Answer: 252

RENAISSANCE EXPRESS, MA'AM. I HAVE A DELIVERY FOR BORGIA.

CURARE

BELLADONNA W/NEWT

HEMLOCK No PRESERVATIVES

ALFREDO SAUCE

Rush Job

In 1849, a man went to the California gold rush hoping to make his fortune by selling tents to the miners. However, the weather was fine and the miners slept out in the open, so the man could sell no tents. But he made his fortune anyway and his name is famous to this day. How did he become rich and who is he?

Clues: 187 /Answer: 252

The Engraving

A woman saw an advertisement for a color engraving of Queen Elizabeth II for $1 and bought it. When it arrived, she had no cause for complaint, but she wasn't pleased. Why?

Clues: 188 /Answer: 252

Who Did It?

A child at school printed something rude on the wall and nobody owned up to doing it. How did the teacher find out who did it?

Clues: 188 /Answer: 252

Lethal Relief

A famine-stricken Third World country was receiving food aid from the West, but this inadvertently led to the deaths of several people. How?

Clues: 188 /Answer: 252

HOT JOB

A man held up a bank on a hot day. He was caught later by the police. On a colder day he would probably not have been caught. Why?

Clues: 188 / Answer: 252

CHOP CHOP

Why was an ancient, rare, and healthy tree that stood well away from all buildings in the grounds of Cork University condemned to be cut down?

Clues: 188 / Answer: 253

RESISTANCE

During the German advance and occupation of France in World War II, how did some French resistance fighters booby-trap rooms in a way that put Germans more at risk than French people?

Clues: 189 / Answer: 253

BASKET CASE

She was responsible for the deaths of many people, yet she was never charged. How come?

Clues: 189 / Answer: 253

INVISIBLE EARNINGS

Nauru, in the South Pacific, has a high income per capita. But its wealth doesn't come from anything it grows, makes, or mines. Where does its wealth come from?

Clues: 189 / Answer: 253

ABSOLUTE MADNESS

Why were 20 sane people put into a mental hospital?

Clues: 189 / Answer: 253

From the World Association of Learning, Laughter, and Youth (WALLY) comes the WALLY Test! It is a set of quick-fire questions. They may look easy, but be warned—they are designed to trick you. Write down your answers on a piece of paper and then see how many you got right. The time limit is three minutes.

1. If a man bets you that he can bite his eye, should you take the bet?
2. If he now bets you that he can bite his other eye, should you take that bet?
3. How can you stand behind someone while he or she stands behind you?
4. What looks like a horse, moves likes a horse, and is as big as a horse but weighs nothing?
5. Who is bigger: Mr. Bigger or Mr. Bigger's son?
6. Tom's mother had three children. One was named April. One was named May. What was the third one named?
7. Where could you go to see an ancient pyramid, an iceberg, and a huge waterfall?
8. What has four fingers and a thumb but isn't a hand?
9. What multiplies by division?
10. What's white when it's dirty and black when it's clean?

Answers: 254

TERRIBLY
TRICKY PUZZLES

SPIES ARE US

During World War I, two German spies often ate at the same restaurant, but they never sat together. How did they pass information?

Clues: 189 /Answer: 254

TITTLE TATTLE

You have seen many tittles in the last few minutes. What are they?

Clues: 190 /Answer: 254

OUTSTANDING

What feature of The Old Farmer's Almanac made it vastly more popular than all its rivals for over 100 years in the rural U.S.?

Clues: 190 /Answer: 255

THE STUFFED CLOUD

A meteorologist was replaced in his job because of a stuffed cloud. What's a stuffed cloud?

Clues: 190 /Answer: 255

A Strange Collection

At a dinner, a small container is passed around the table and every guest puts something in it. The contents are then thrown away. What's going on?

Clues: 190 / Answer: 255

Foreign Cure

Why does an American fly to another country in the hope of finding a cure for his illness?

Clues: 190 / Answer: 255

Bus Lane Bonus

A city introduced bus lanes on busy streets and the death rate dropped quickly. Why?

Clues: 191 /Answer: 255

Blow by Blow

Why was a man at a fairground blowing darts through a concealed blowpipe?

Clues: 191 /Answer: 255

History Question

What happened in London on September 8, 1752?

Clues: 191 /Answer: 256

Sign Here

A man bought two identical signs but found that he could use only one of them. Why?

Clues: 191 /Answer: 256

Paper Tiger

A man writes the same number, and nothing else, on 20 sheets of paper. Why?

Clues: 191 /Answer: 256

Forging Ahead

A forger went into a store with a genuine $50 bill. How did he use this to come out with a $20 profit?

Clues: 192 /Answer: 256

Smile Please!

A man wrote to a toothpaste company suggesting a way in which they could significantly increase their sales. How?

Clues: 192 /Answer: 256

High on a Hill

A man was marooned overnight on a mountain above the snow line in winter. He had no protective clothing and no tent. How did he survive?

Clues: 192 / Answer: 256

Mine Shafted

In order to sell it, a con man salted a useless mine with a number of genuine pieces of silver. How did the buyer figure out the scheme?

Clues: 192 / Answer: 257

THAT WILL TEACH YOU

One day a man came home to collect something he had forgotten, and found that his house had been completely destroyed. What had happened?

Clues: 192 /Answer: 257

A GEOGRAPHY QUESTION

Which states of the U.S. are the most western, most southern, most northern, and most eastern?

Clues: 193 /Answer: 257

THE GENEROUS GENERAL

A retired English general was saddened to see a beggar on the street with a sign reading "World War II veteran." So he gave him £10. The man thanked him and the general became angry. Why?

Clues: 193 / Answer: 257

FAST MOVER!

How did a man with an out-of-date passport legitimately visit 30 different countries in the same day?

Clues: 193 / Answer: 257

RUNNING ON EMPTY

Mrs. Jones was very pleased that the car ran out of gas. Why?

Clues: 193 / Answer: 257

WHAT'S THE POINT?

Why does a woman always use a square pencil in the course of her work?

Clues: 193 / Answer: 258

THE OFFICE JOB

A man applied for a job in an office. When he arrived at the busy, noisy office he was told by the receptionist to fill out a form and then wait until called. He completed the form and then sat and waited along with four other candidates who had arrived earlier. After a few minutes, he got up and went into an inner office and was subsequently given the job. The other candidates who had arrived earlier were angry. The manager explained why the man had been given the job. What was the reason?

Clues: 193 / Answer: 258

HEARTY APPETITE

A whale ate normally and many people were very disappointed. Why?

Clues: 194 / Answer: 258

THE UPSET BIRD WATCHER

A keen ornithologist saw a rare bird that he had never seen before, except in illustrations. However, he was very upset. Then he was frightened. Why?

Clues: 194 /Answer: 258

FLOATING HOME

A man went on a long trip and was gone several weeks. When he returned, he was found floating at sea. How come?

Clues: 194 /Answer: 258

CO-LATERAL DAMAGE

During World War II, U.S. forces lost many bombers in raids over Germany due to antiaircraft fire. From the damage on returning bombers, they were able to build up a clear picture of which parts of the planes were hit most frequently and which weren't hit at all. How did they use this information to reduce losses?

Clues: 194 /Answer: 258

ORSON CART

When Orson Welles caused nationwide panic with his radio broadcast of the Martian landing, there was one group that wasn't fooled. Who were they?

Clues: 194 /Answer: 259

THROWING HIS WEIGHT ABOUT

Why did a man who was not suicidal and not threatened in any way throw himself through a plate-glass window on the 24th floor of an office building and so fall to his death?

Clues: 195 /Answer: 259

DISCONNECTED?

A horse walked all day. Two of its legs traveled 21 miles and two legs traveled 20 miles. How come?

Clues: 195 /Answer: 259

Joker

Four people were playing cards. One played a card and another player immediately jumped up and started to take her clothes off. Why?

Clues: 195 / Answer: 260

Rich Man, Poor Man

In England, why did rich people pour their tea first and then add milk while poor people poured milk first and then added tea?

Clues: 196 / Answer: 260

Mined Over Matter

A sailor at the bow of his ship saw a mine floating in the water directly in the path of the vessel. There was no time to change the ship's direction. How did he avert disaster?

Clues: 196 / Answer: 260

SURPRISE VISIT

A factory manager gets a tip that the company chairman is on his way to pay a surprise visit. The manager orders the staff to clean the factory, clear out all the trash, and hide it away, but the chairman wasn't impressed. Why not?

Clues: 196 /Answer: 260

SCHOOL'S OUT

Why does an elderly lady receive a court order to go to school immediately?

Clues: 196 /Answer: 260

THE DEADLY STONE

A man shot himself because he saw a stone with a small drop of blood on it. Why?

Clues: 196 /Answer: 260

THE COSTLY WAVE

A man waved his hands in the air and this action cost him $30,000. Why?

Clues: 197 /Answer: 261

WALLY Test IV

Time for another WALLY Test. The questions may look easy, but be warned—they're designed to trip you up. Write down your answers on a piece of paper and then see how many you got right. The time limit is three minutes.

1. What gets higher as it falls?
2. How do you stop moles from digging in your garden?
3. Why did the overweight actor fall through the theater floor?
4. What happened to the man who invented the silent alarm clock?
5. What's the best known star with a tail?
6. How did an actor get his name up in lights in every theater in the country?
7. Where would you find a square ring?
8. What do you give a bald rabbit?
9. How do you make a slow horse fast?
10. Why did Sam wear a pair of pants with three large holes?

Answers: 261

TREMENDOUSLY TRICKY PUZZLES

2020 VISION

A newspaper editor heard a report that 2020 pigs had been stolen from a farm, so he called the farmer to check the story. The farmer told him the same story, but the editor changed the number for insertion in the news. Why?

Clues: 197 / Answer: 261

THE DEADLY OMELET

A man went into a country inn and ordered an omelet for lunch. He was promptly arrested and later executed. Why?

Clues: 197 / Answer: 262

THE GAP

A man was writing the word HIM. Why did he deliberately leave a gap between the final two letters so that it looked a little like HI M?

Clues: 197 / Answer: 262

THE DINNER CLUE

A suspect is interrogated for several hours but doesn't crack. He then demands a meal and soon afterward the police charge him with murder. Why?

Clues: 197 /Answer: 262

WRONG WAY

Why does a man who wants to catch a bus going from Alewife to Zebedee deliberately catch one going the opposite way—from Zebedee to Alewife?

Clues: 197 /Answer: 262

THE SINGLE WORD

A woman whom I had never met before was introduced to me. I didn't say a word. She told me about herself, but I didn't say a word. She told me many more things about herself, but I didn't say a word. Eventually I said one word and she was very disappointed. What was the word?

Clues: 198 /Answer: 262

THE MAN WHO WOULD NOT READ

A tourist in England was traveling by train. He had a book with him that he wanted to read, but he didn't start it until he got off the train. Why?

Clues: 198 /Answer: 263

NOT EATING?

A hungry man has food on his plate but doesn't eat it. Why?

Clues: 198 / Answer: 263

TWO PIGS

A farmer has two pigs that are identical twins from the same litter. However, when he sells them he gets 100 times more for one than the other. Why?

Clues: 198 / Answer: 263

Eensy Weensy Spider Farm

In some parts of France there are spider farms. Why would anybody want to farm spiders?

Clues: 199 /Answer: 263

I'LL HAVE THE SNAILS, THE CALF'S BRAIN AND PANCREAS, AND FOR DESSERT, THE CHOCOLATE BLACK WIDOW CAKE.

Face-off

In World War I, the French and Austrian armies faced each other. Neither side attacked the other nor fired a shot at the other, yet thousands were killed. How?

Clues: 199 /Answer: 263

A man at a party is offered a choice of a certain food—either the expensive fresh variety or the cheaper canned variety. Why does he choose the cheaper canned food?

Clues: 199 / Answer: 263

UP IN SMOKE

A man owned some excellent cigars, which he smoked. As a result of this he gained $10,000 and a prison sentence. How?

Clues: 199 / Answer: 264

SILLY CONE

How did an office manager achieve greater efficiency using cones?

Clues: 199 /Answer: 264

NOT THE FÜHRER

A body that looked very like that of Adolf Hitler was found by advancing Allied troops near Hitler's bunker in Berlin. The face was destroyed. How did the soldiers quickly find out that it wasn't Hitler's body?

Clues: 200 /Answer: 264

Vase and Means

How did the ancient potters discover the ingredient that made perfect china?

Clues: 200 / Answer: 264

My Condiments to the Chef

Why did the owner of a café replace all the bottles of condiments on his tables with packets?

Clues: 200 / Answer: 264

The Man Who Did Not Fly

Why was a fictitious name added to an airline's passenger list?

Clues: 200 / Answer: 265

Inheritance

In ancient Ireland, a king had two sons, each of whom wanted to inherit the kingdom. The king decreed that each should be put in a separate rowboat about one mile from shore and told to row in. The first to touch the shore would inherit the kingdom. The elder and stronger son rowed more quickly and was about to touch the shore with the younger son some 20 yards behind him and farther out to sea. How did the younger son inherit the kingdom?

Clues: 200 / Answer: 265

STAMP DEARTH DEATH

A man died because he didn't buy enough stamps. What happened?

Clues: 201 /Answer: 265

ROCK OF AGES

A man suffered a serious injury because he was listening to rock-and-roll music. What happened?

Clues: 201 /Answer: 265

QUO VADIS?

How was an archaeologist in Britain able to deduce that the Romans drove their chariots on the left-hand side of the road?

Clues: 201 /Answer: 266

Pork Puzzler

Why did a man who didn't like bacon always pack some bacon when he went on a trip, and throw it out when he arrived?

Clues: 201 /Answer: 266

Frozen Assets

Why did they build a railway line over the ice when the place could be reached by land and they knew the ice would melt anyway?

Clues: 201 /Answer: 266

TURNED OFF

A man inadvertently caused all radio station transmissions in the world to cease. How? And who was he?

Clues: 202 /Answer: 266

THE LAST MAIL

A man mailed two letters to the same address at the same time in the same post office. The letters were identical but the postage on one letter was more than on the other. Why?

Clues: 202 /Answer: 266

SMALL IS NOT BEAUTIFUL

Why were small cars banned in Sweden?

Clues: 202 / Answer: 267

THE DEADLY FEATHER

A man lies dead next to a feather that caused his death. What happened?

Clues: 202 / Answer: 267

THE SEALED ROOM

A perfectly healthy man was trapped in a sealed room. He died, but not from lack of oxygen. What did he die of?

Clues: 203 / Answer: 267

WRITTEN DOWN

A woman is writing in capital letters. She has difficulty writing the letters A, E, F, G, H, and L, but no difficulty with C, K, M, N, V, and W. Why?

Clues: 203 /Answer: 267

PUBLICITY PUZZLER

A man put an ad in the newspaper. As a result of this, he and another man go shopping together twice a year, but have no other contact. Why?

Clues: 203 /Answer: 267

Who Wants It Anyway?

He who has it is worried. He who loses it is poorer. He who wins it no longer has it. What is it?

Clues: 203 /Answer: 268

Knights of Old

What action carried out by knights because of their armor has persisted to this day, when no one wears armor?

Clues: 203 /Answer: 268

Shave That Pig!

"Barber, Barber, shave a pig" goes an old nursery rhyme. Why would anyone want to shave a live pig?

Clues: 204 /Answer: 268

WATCH OUT!

A man left his house to get a drink but died because his watch stopped. Why?

Clues: 204 / Answer: 269

THE WEDDING PRESENT

A man bought a beautiful and appropriate wedding gift for a friend's wedding. The gift was wrapped and sent. When the gift was opened at the wedding, the man was highly embarrassed. Why?

Clues: 204 / Answer: 269

A woman murders her husband. She gains no advantage for herself in doing so. The police knew she did it. She was never charged with murder. What was going on?

Clues: 204 /Answer: 269

CLUES

BATTY BANDITRY

Welcome, Slasher

Q: Were the boy and the policeman what they appeared to be and not, for example, actors for a movie?
A: Yes.
Q: Was the policeman honest?
A: Yes.
Q: Did the boy act in retaliation, perhaps to deter a criminal who could not be prosecuted by normal methods?
A: No.

Smashed Taillights

Q: Did the owner give Bob permission to smash the taillights?
A: No.
Q: Had the car been stolen?
A: No.
Q: After the taillights were smashed, was something important revealed behind them?
A: Yes.

Supposed to Kill?

Q: Did the intended victim run or call for help?
A: No.
Q: Having learned that the gun was not loaded, did anyone try to grab it or otherwise forcibly intervene?
A: No.

Q: The incident did not result in death or serious injury. Did anyone want it to?

A: No.

BURNING DOWN THE BUILDING

Q: Did anyone bribe the landlord?

A: No.

Q: Did the fire destroy evidence of a crime?

A: No.

Q: Did a tenant set the fire, perhaps out of anger?

A: No.

CAUGHT IN THE ACT

Q: Was he really a pickpocket?

A: Yes.

Q: Did he want to be arrested?

A: No.

Q: Did he act rationally?

A: Yes.

SLIPPERY SIDNEY SLIPPED UP

Q: Had Sidney tried to sell the rented car by forging a title to it?

A: No.

Q: Did Sidney return the car intact and drivable, with no collision damage and no replacement of good major parts with inferior ones?

A: Yes.

Q: Was the fraud obvious to the rental-car company, but only after at least a month had passed?

A: Yes.

HONEST IVAN

Q: Had Ivan wanted to use the car for at least two months, including driving back to Florida for a vacation with his family?

A: Yes.

Q: Did Ivan cause the collision that damaged the car or contribute to it in any way?

A: No.

Q: Had Ivan creatively reacted to the difference between auto insurance rates in Florida and those in Washington, D.C., where he lived?

A: Yes.

ROBBING THE BANK

Q: Was the tip-off about the paychecks correct?

A: Yes.

Q: Did the bank have more cash on hand then than usual?

A: Yes.

Q: Did the robbers obtain any cash?

A: No.

HE CALLED THE POLICE

Q: Did he call a co-conspirator on the police force?

A: No.

Q: Before breaking in, had he intended to call the police?

A: No.

Q: Was he arrested?

A: Yes.

ARRESTED ANYWAY

Q: Was Rocky wanted for a previous crime?
A: No.
Q: Did Rocky have to change planes?
A: Yes.
Q: When Rocky checked his suitcase, did he expect it to be delivered directly to his final destination?
A: No.

NO RANSOM DEMAND

Q: Was the man rational, even though his actions seem inexplicable?
A: Yes.
Q: Is it significant that he was able to bring a firearm past a metal detector?
A: Yes.
Q: Did the man have an accomplice, perhaps someone who was able to sneak a gun into the building for him?
A: No.

ESCAPING THE KIDNAPPERS

Q: Did Brenda get a dial tone, even though the phone had a rotary dial that couldn't be used?
A: Yes.
Q: Did she untie herself, or was she somehow able to break or remove the dial lock?
A: No.
Q: Did she use the telephone?
A: Yes.

PEOPLE PUZZLES

HEARING THEM QUICKLY

Q: Was the father telling the truth?
A: Yes.
Q: Did he intend to keep Dana from hearing the concert?
A: No.
Q: Is it significant that the father was reading the TV listings at the time?
A: Yes.

MOTORCYCLE MADNESS

Q: Did Amy know those particular motorcyclists?
A: No.
Q: Was she as angry at the motorcyclist trespassers as were Jamie and Peter?
A: Yes.
Q: Did the motorcyclists who managed to escape know Peter or his jeep?
A: No.

A CRYING PROBLEM

Q: Did Sandra or her parents-in-law mention any painful subjects or otherwise depart from casual conversation?
A: No.
Q: When her husband's parents said that they were happy for the telephone call, were they telling the truth?
A: Yes.
Q: Did Sandra explain her motive for making the call?
A: No.

SHE NEVER FIXED HIM UP

Q: Was Mitch genuinely interested in a blind date?
A: Yes.
Q: Did he trust Anna's judgment?
A: Yes.
Q: Was Mitch transferred or reassigned to a kind of work in which a social life would be unconventional or impossible?
A: No.

HAPPY THAT SHE CURSED HIM

Q: Was the man a masochist, who generally liked being unpleasantly treated?
A: No.
Q: Did the woman love him?
A: Yes.
Q: Did he believe that her angry words were really directed at him?
A: No.

EVICTED

Q: Did the son live in the father's house?
A: Yes.
Q: Was there a physical danger in the house from which the father wanted to protect his son?
A: No.
Q: Did the father own the house and unquestionably have the legal right to have his son live with him (son not a fugitive from justice, etc.)?
A: Yes.

CRAZY CARS AND TRICKY TRANSPORT

DRIVING THE WRONG CAR

Q: Did each car have a hitch and compatible bumper, allowing either car to tow the other awhile if both worked?
A: Yes.
Q: Was the broken car smashed so it would not tow easily?
A: No.
Q: Was the only problem with the broken car related to its brakes, so the other car could be towed with its brakes partially set?
A: No.

SAFE SMASH-UP

Q: Was the car controlled by a radio-operated device, as for a movie?
A: No.
Q: Was the car deliberately damaged?
A: No.
Q: Did the car catch fire after its fuel line burst?
A: No.

CONTAGIOUS CARSICKNESS?

Q: Was there something wrong with the car?
A: No.
Q: When Jan felt sick, were they all breathing fresh air?
A: Yes.
Q: Were they then outside the car?
A: Yes.

What Drained the Battery?

Q: When Walter returned to the car, was anything switched on or the hood open?

A: No.

Q: Had anyone been in the parking lot since Walter parked his car and ran inside?

A: Yes.

Q: Did Walter lock his car?

A: No.

Seasonal Mileage

Q: Does the answer have to do with snow on the ground or snow tires on the car?

A: No.

Q: Does Claude drive along exactly the same roads in summer as in winter, and in the same car?

A: Yes.

Q: Are the windows open in summer, causing much more wind resistance, until closed at the end of a trip?

A: No.

SHE ARRIVED ON TIME

Q: Could Carol have driven from home to the coffeehouse in two minutes, at less than a hundred miles per hour?

A: No.

Q: Did she use unusual transportation, such as a helicopter?

A: No.

Q: Did Daryl dial her home number correctly and reach her by doing so?

A: Yes.

A TOKEN WAIT IN A TOKEN LINE

Q: Did Smart Stephanie have someone buy her tokens, or go to the subway station at odd, "off-peak" hours?

A: No.

Q: Did she sneak under turnstiles, otherwise evade the fare, or have permission to use the subway without paying (as can some police officers, subway employees, and such)?

A: No.

Q: Did she live in a strictly residential district and work in a strictly business district during ordinary business hours?

A: Yes.

THE LATE TRAIN

Q: Does the lateness have anything to do with the train's having crossed from one time zone to another?

A: No.

Q: At the time Amanda stepped onto the train, did its crew expect it to become late before she got off it?

A: Yes.

Q: Could this incident, for this reason, happen only at a particular time of year?

A: Yes.

ODD OFFICES

STUBBORN STEVE

Q: Did Steve choose paper that was multiple-part, tractor-feed, or otherwise special or unusual?

A: No.

Q: Was the sales clerk completely honest and accurate?

A: Yes.

Q: Was the paper intended for an exotic use that was not reasonably expected by its manufacturer, such as papier-mâché or analysis under a microscope?

A: No.

MAKING THE GRADE

Q: Did Nell want a good grade on the course, so that she was planning to have her paper properly written and handed in on or before the deadline?

A: Yes.

Q: Did she have any reason to doubt the receptionist?

A: No.

Q: Is her straight-A average, which suggests good study habits, significant?

A: Yes.

SPACED-OUT AT THE COMPUTER

Q: Can it be done, in general, with only one "replace" command?

A: No.

Q: Can it be done by typing the same "replace" command over and over again?

A: Yes.

Q: Is there another way to solve the problem, one that involves typing three different commands?

A: Yes.

THE FAST ELEVATOR TRIP

Q: Was the elevator working properly and able to go to the floor where Bill had his appointment?

A: Yes.

Q: Was Bill prevented from getting on, as by a work crew loading a piece of heavy machinery?

A: No.

Q: Did Bill correctly reason that he would get to his appointment faster by not using that elevator?

A: Yes.

THE NONSTOP ELEVATOR TRIP

Q: Were they on a high floor in an office building?

A: Yes.

Q: Did the building have separate groups of elevators to serve separate ranges of floors?

A: Yes.

Q: Could anyone get into a crowded elevator on the ground floor and reasonably expect to get directly to the floor where Bill was, without having the elevator stop at other floors first?

A: No.

TOO PRECISE

Q: Did Jerry and Mary correctly think that vagueness was generally believed important to their business?

A: Yes.

Q: Did they intend to bring profit to their boss?
A: No.
Q: Were they paid for their work?
A: No.

EXCEPTIONALLY VAGUE

Q: Did Mary want part of the candidate's political platform to be obscured for any reason?
A: No.
Q: Was it part of a press release or internal memorandum?
A: No.
Q: Did it consist of ten or fewer words?
A: Yes.

THE HOSTILE VOTER

Q: Had Charlie decided whom to vote for before receiving the call?
A: No.
Q: Did he think that the volunteer told the truth?
A: Yes.
Q: Did he notice an inconsistency in what the volunteer said that alerted him to a problem?
A: Yes.

A MYSTERY FAX

Q: Was the call a wrong or misdialed number?
A: No.
Q: If the executive had anticipated the call and connected a fax machine to his telephone line, then would the fax call have resulted in his receiving a fax transmission?
A: No.

Q: Did the executive know who or what originated the fax call?

A: Yes.

ANOTHER MYSTERY FAX

Q: Was the fax a real one, intended to be received and read just like an ordinary fax, with no codes or secret messages involved?

A: Yes.

Q: Did the colleague prefer or insist on a fax in preference to an ordinary phone call, perhaps because of deafness?

A: No.

Q: Did the content of the fax include any tables or other lengthy material that is more easily explained in writing than by speaking?

A: No.

PROBLEMS WITH PERSONNEL

Q: Had the friend seen the advertisement?

A: Yes.

Q: Had the friend followed its instructions and applied for the position?

A: Yes.

Q: Did the personnel department exactly follow the instructions that Raymond had given?

A: Yes.

MORE PROBLEMS WITH PERSONNEL

Q: Did the colleague and the new person conspire to defraud Raymond's company?

A: No.

Q: Was the colleague thoroughly honest?

A: Yes.

Q: Although the reference-checking turned up no evidence of a problem, was the newly hired person honest?

A: No.

DISMAYING DIZZINESS

Q: Was the dizziness caused by fumes from office machinery or any other source, or related to any toxic substance?

A: No.

Q: If the office had not had the listed changes, then would dizziness result from being in it?

A: No.

Q: Would the dizziness probably be worse after sunset than at midday?

A: Yes.

ASININE ACTIONS

GIVING WAYNE THE BOOT

Q: Were the police officers honest and Wayne's neighbor not politically influential?

A: Yes.

Q: Was it the same person who turned on the loud music and threw the boot through Wayne's window?

A: Yes.

Q: Was the neighbor happy when the police arrived?

A: Yes.

Racing the Drawbridge

Q: Was Clarence sensible?
A: Yes.
Q: Did he turn away or stop?
A: No.
Q: If the drawbridge was closed, then would Clarence have approached the bridge?
A: No.

Recycled Salt

Q: Are we talking about ordinary table salt, sodium chloride?
A: Yes.
Q: Is the salt eaten?
A: Yes.
Q: Is the same salt eaten twice?
A: Yes.

Scared of Her Shadow?

Q: Does the sun shine brightly in Florida?
A: Yes.
Q: Is the reason for opening a car window concerned with controlling the temperature in the car?
A: No.
Q: When the sun is shining brightly behind a car, which is not the same as shining in a driver's eyes, is there potential danger because something important cannot be seen?
A: Yes.

PICTURE THE TOURISTS

Q: Did Sherman want to change places so that he would get better pictures for himself?

A: No.

Q: Was Sherman originally sitting next to a window?

A: Yes.

Q: Was the window open?

A: No.

THE MIRROR

Q: Is the mirror placed where anyone could look directly into it easily?

A: No.

Q: Is it made from ordinary plate glass?

A: No.

Q: Is it the only mirror that is mounted near the bed?

A: No.

THE EMPTY WRAPPER

Q: Was the incident an attempt to cheat the customer, or related to fraud in any context?

A: No.

Q: Did the woman who removed the wrapper from the cart know that the wrapper was empty?

A: Yes.

Q: Was the woman accompanied while she shopped?

A: Yes.

Q: Was the gasoline adulterated, the wrong octane rating, or otherwise intended to make the car run poorly?

A: No.

Q: Did the neighbor know of Marvin's activities?

A: No.

Q: Was the car covered by a warranty?

A: Yes.

FORGOT TO STOP?

Q: One minute before Angus jumped out of the car, did he expect to do so?

A: No.

Q: After he jumped out of the car, did he expect to get into it again?

A: No.

Q: Did more than two minutes pass between when Angus jumped out of the car and when he reached the ground?

A: Yes.

Short-Lived Messages

Q: Does she show them to someone else, perhaps because they are cue cards for a newscaster?

A: No.

Q: Are the messages intermediate steps in mathematical calculations or part of the process of encoding secret data?

A: No.

Q: Are they intermediate steps in an electronic message-handling process that is familiar to the public?

A: Yes.

More Short-Lived Writing

Q: Are computers or any other electronic devices involved?

A: No.

Q: By what she is doing, does she intend to communicate to anyone?

A: No.

Q: Although it is immediately erased, does her output from the writing instrument in turn help erase something else?

A: Yes.

HAPHAZARD HAPPENINGS

The Mail Is In!

Q: Had Oscar put the order form into the outgoing mail slot next to the mailboxes the previous day, after that day's mail had been delivered?

A: Yes.

Q: Did the mailboxes have big pods nearby, so that a mail carrier could put a parcel in one of them and the key to that pod in that resident's mailbox?

A: Yes.

Q: Did Oscar pay particular attention to the pods?

A: Yes.

MAGAZINE SUBSCRIPTIONS

Q: Could the need anticipated by those who save them be satisfied by blank paper of similar size and shape?

A: No.

Q: Are they used to cause troublesome paperwork by writing someone else's name on them and then mailing them?

A: No.

Q: Is their reply-paid status very important, more so than for an ordinary postcard?

A: Yes.

SOLICITING IN SEATTLE

Q: Do the two friends have similar age and ethnicity, live in similar single-family houses, and live in neighborhoods that, though not close to each other, have virtually identical demographic statistics?

A: Yes.

Q: Is the explanation related to an anti-canvassing ordinance that affects one neighborhood but not the other?

A: No.

Q: Can the difference be traced to the personal convenience of the canvassers?

A: Yes.

IT'S A DOG'S LIFE

Q: Was the healthy-looking dog less than five years old and truly healthy and uninjured?
A: Yes.
Q: Were both dogs owned by the same owner?
A: Yes.
Q: If not for its serious injuries, would the puppy be expected to live for more than one month?
A: No.

NOT FROM THE USA

Q: He was not from the USA, but would he necessarily speak English with a recognizably foreign accent?
A: No.
Q: Was he referring to dry non-USA land, and not an island?
A: Yes.
Q: Could the USA be reached by traveling less than 150 miles north, south, east or west from one point in his home country?
A: Yes.

DOTS ON THE I'S

Q: Is a small I with a dot over it commonly seen?
A: No.
Q: If Timmy had written his statement, instead of spoken it, then would the puzzle be easy?
A: Yes.
Q: In his retort, was Timmy talking about the same thing that Jimmy had teased him about earlier?
A: No.

Power Failure

Q: Did Horace sleep away from his house and return to it to find the clocks all stopped?
A: No.
Q: Was he of sound mind and with good vision?
A: Yes.
Q: Did he own an electric clock that had an hour hand and a minute hand?
A: No.

Afraid of the Country

Q: Is Nicolai's background significant?
A: Yes.
Q: Had be been subjected to mistreatment or tortured on a farm in Russia?
A: No.
Q: Would he have enjoyed visiting an actual livestock farm?
A: Yes.

Long-Life Bulbs

Q: Were the bulbs totally ordinary?
A: Yes.
Q: The ordinary incandescent bulbs screwed into ordinary sockets, but could a fluorescent bulb that had a socket base and that fit into the fixtures be used instead?
A: No.
Q: Does the answer have to do with the structure of incandescent bulbs?
A: Yes.

Q: Did Ted intend to give Ned practice at running to catch a high ball?

A: No.

Q: Could Ted have aimed the ball directly at Ned if he had wanted to?

A: Yes.

Q: Is their location significant?

A: Yes.

Ballpark Befuddlement

Q: Was the man unhappy with the results of the first two swings?

A: Yes.

Q: Did the final ball go over a fence?

A: No.

Q: Did the man run after the third swing?

A: No.

CRASS CREDITORS AND DULL DEBTORS

Overdue Payment

Q: Did Jim use ordinary first-class mail and only first-class mail?

A: Yes.

Q: He reduced the chance of his payment being late because of a postal delay, but did he eliminate it completely?

A: No.

Q: Is it important that Jim sent a payment every month?
A: Yes.

WRONG ORDER

Q: Did Jim mail both checks, in separate envelopes with ordinary first-class postage, to the same address, from the same town, on the same day?
A: Yes.
Q: Did he mail the lower-numbered check first?
A: Yes.
Q: Did he put both checks into mailboxes?
A: No.

I'VE GOT YOUR NUMBER

Q: Did Kingfist obtain the telephone number from confederates at the phone company or from Sam's friends?
A: No.
Q: Did he enter the house?
A: No.
Q: Is the fact that Sam's fence was climbable significant?
A: Yes.

COLLECTING BACKWARDS

Q: Was the check for more than the debt?
A: No.
Q: Was the deposit made in cash?
A: Yes.
Q: Would Kingfist have preferred not to have made the deposit?
A: Yes.

BETTER LATE THAN PROMPT

Q: If the debtor would have honored the original contract, then would Kingfist have offered the new one?

A: No.

Q: Did Kingfist collect more readily under the new contract than under the old one?

A: Yes.

Q: Did Kingfist collect completely legally?

A: Yes.

THE DEBTOR PAID

Q: Was Kingfist the actual creditor, not a collection agent for someone else?

A: Yes.

Q: Can a creditor use collection methods that a collection agent cannot?

A: Yes.

Q: Did Kingfist receive any of the money that was collected?

A: No.

DAFFY DOCTORING

SHE WAS IN THE HOSPITAL

Q: Did Alan and his wife genuinely love each other?

A: Yes.

Q: Nevertheless, was Alan pleased with the news?

A: Yes.

Q: Would his wife have been happy if Alan had tried to visit her when she left the operating room?

A: No.

APPENDICITIS

Q: Does removing the appendix make appendicitis permanently impossible?
A: Yes.
Q: Did the physician confuse Zeke with someone else or otherwise remember incorrectly?
A: No.
Q: When the physician responded to the call and saw Zeke's wife, did he instantly consider appendicitis even before examining her?
A: Yes.

CROSSED VISION

Q: Can you improve your vision by crossing your fingers behind your back?
A: No.
Q: Can everyone benefit from crossing the fingers?
A: No.
Q: Do you need to do something with your crossed fingers?
A: Yes.

NIGHT BLINDNESS CURE

Q: Is medical knowledge necessary to ask the questions or interpret the answers?
A: No.
Q: Are drugs or nutritional supplements needed?
A: No.
Q: Is the setting in which night blindness occurs important?
A: Yes.

A Sweet Problem

Q: Is the sugar swallowed?

A: No.

Q: Can another common substance substitute for the sugar?

A: No.

Q: Under specified conditions, can the sugar be similarly used by people who are not diabetic?

A: Yes.

Miracle Cures

Q: Is the additional explanation known to those to whom it applies?

A: Yes.

Q: When that explanation applies to someone, does it always work?

A: Yes.

Q: After it works, can it ever be identified, even with exhaustive medical tests and scientific scrutiny?

A: No.

Not a Trusted Doctor

Q: Are apparent cures for senility likely to be fraudulent?

A: Yes.

Q: Did Cassandra have any reason to believe the diploma to be counterfeit, borrowed, or stolen?

A: No.

Q: Did the boyfriend know much about Cassandra's past?

A: No.

The Plumber's Pressure

Q: Was the plumber's occupation relevant?
A: Yes.
Q: Was his reasoning correct?
A: Yes.
Q: Was the plumber's earlier ailment a common one?
A: Yes.

Rx Lead Poisoning

Q: Would lead poisoning, the only foreseen consequence of eating lead-based paint, have helped treat the ailment?
A: No.
Q: If not for the fact that his patient was covered by insurance, would there be any reason for the doctor's strange suggestion?
A: No.
Q: Did the doctor intend to treat the lead poisoning?
A: Yes.

Long Walk for the Disabled

Q: Did he park farther to walk more, for the sake of exercise?
A: No.
Q: Did he need to drive another kind of vehicle, perhaps giving up an easily parked bicycle or motorcycle and driving a car instead?
A: No.
Q: Did he own a car and have to alter it because of his injury?
A: Yes.

ECCENTRIC ELECTRONICS

Happy with the TV Ad

Q: Had an accomplice damaged the television station, its transmitter, or anything related to it?

A: No.

Q: Did the man hope to sell diagnostic television repair services or TV sets?

A: No.

Q: Would he have been pleased if the test pattern had appeared at a different time or on another channel?

A: No.

Time for Repairs

Q: Did the watch work properly, even though Dilton at first didn't think it did?

A: Yes.

Q: Earlier, had Dilton properly set it to the correct time?

A: Yes.

Q: When Dilton noticed something wrong, was the watch showing an incorrect time from running too fast or slow?

A: No.

Strange Sounds

Q: Are the sounds and pictures out of sync, as when words on a foreign-language film don't match the speaker's lips?

A: No.

Q: Do mistimed sounds—too early or late—give it away?

A: No.

Q: Are some sounds inappropriately absent?
A: Yes.

WATCHING THE GAME

Q: Did Elmer use an illegally manufactured descrambler?
A: No.
Q: Did he have an accomplice at a television station or at a satellite company?
A: No.
Q: Did he have a noncompeting accomplice who ran another sports bar?
A: Yes.

DIGITAL DOWNFALL

Q: Do such disks have more background noise than non-digital media or supply the wrong frequency, as can warped vinyl records?
A: No.
Q: Are the enthusiasts concerned only with not replacing their older electronic devices?
A: No.
Q: Can the enthusiasts trace their preference to a scientifically credible explanation?
A: Yes.

THE TV OBEYED

Q: Did Jake shout to operate a sound-sensitive switch or, while shouting, manually operate a remote-control device or an ordinary switch?
A: No.
Q: Did Jake see the television screen just before he shouted?

A: Yes.

Q: Videotaped movies usually have their durations print-ed on their boxes. Is that fact significant?

A: Yes.

The VCR Timers

Q: Is the device's nightly programming ability significant?

A: Yes.

Q: Was the new VCR regularly used to record anything else?

A: No.

Q: Was the hardware store purchase used to alter or dis-assemble anything?

A: No.

The VCR Remote Control

Q: Did Jenny have or know about a different remote con-trol, perhaps a wall one or one otherwise dog-resistant?

A: No.

Q: Was the television beyond the foot of the bed, well out of reach of someone lying in it?

A: Yes.

Q: Was there something important about the bed?

A: Yes.

No Television Trouble

Q: Is it legal for a television set to be operated so that the driver of a moving motor vehicle can see its screen?

A: No.

Q: Did Stuart know the state trooper, bribe him, or have any special influence?

A: No.

Q: Did Stuart hear the theme music in stereo?

A: Yes.

Inefficiency Pays Off

Q: Does the difference in effectiveness relate to reliability or to relative availability of parts in case of a breakdown?

A: No.

Q: Is an expensive model of the object significantly more likely to be stolen than a cheaper one, making the cheaper one preferable in high-crime areas?

A: No.

Q: Can the elaborate controls be more easily misused than the simple ones?

A: No.

MAD MONEY

Worth Twenty Dollars

Q: Were some United States currency issues redeemable for gold or silver?

A: Yes.

Q: Could Nick, observing that the Federal Reserve issued the bill, exchange it at a Federal Reserve office?

A: Yes.

Q: Are all United States currency notes legal tender in payment of debts?

A: Yes.

Slow-Witted Customers

Q: Is the policy based on deception or misleading advertising, or otherwise actually or potentially illegal?

A: No.

Q: Are coupons, other marketing devices, or passwords acquired elsewhere required to qualify for special savings?

A: No.

Q: Is this policy, by its nature, impossible to use other than by a fast-food restaurant?

A: Yes.

Banking on the Boycott

Q: Had the fast-food chain borrowed money from the bank?

A: No.

Q: Would the man's idea work only if many people took part?

A: Yes.

Q: Was any law broken?

A: No.

OLD MONEY BUT GOOD MONEY

Q: Were the changes deliberately made simultaneously and with the same intent?

A: No.

Q: Did exactly one of them affect the ideology of why money is considered valuable?

A: Yes.

Q: Was the other considered desirable by some conservatives and ironic by others?

A: Yes.

SECRET BUSINESS

Q: Did they use scramblers because they suspected that their telephones were tapped?

A: Yes.

Q: In this particular context, would the secure scramblers, which were compatible with each other, have been as useful as the ones that they actually used?

A: No.

Q: Did the men discuss all of their plans on the telephone?

A: No.

GAS-STATION GLITCH

Q: Was the attendant who announced the five-dollar limit telling the truth?

A: Yes.

Q: Did George, after receiving fuel, receive five dollars in change from the attendant?

A: No.

Q: Was George likely to be one of several angry customers at the gas station?

A: Yes.

MARKETING MUDDLE

Q: Is the car a recent model in the USA?

A: Yes.

Q: Would the name provoke concern if it was displayed, in advertising, only with ordinary letters?

A: No.

Q: Is knowledge of a foreign alphabet important?

A: Yes.

EASY MONEY

Q: Would Butch keep his word and deliver one complete and working television set for each $30 you paid him?

A: Yes.

Q: Did he obtain the set from the inventory that had cost his employer $45 each?

A: Yes.

Q: Did Butch lose money on the transaction?

A: No.

TOO MUCH MONEY

Q: Had the investor any reason to suspect shady financing, a conflict of interest, fraud, or anything even remotely dishonest?

A: No.

Q: Would the investor, as a limited partner, give up control of the investment if someone else invested more than he did?

A: No.

Q: Was the money that stopped the investor from investing money that was already invested in the company, or was going to be invested in it later?

A: No.

GOOFY GAMBLING

LOTTERY LOGIC

Q: Does it have anything to do with the practice of paying lottery winners in monthly or semi-annual installments?

A: No.

Q: Can lottery tickets be a sensible investment, despite their payouts being biased against their purchasers?

A: Yes.

Q: Are they a good investment for everyone?

A: No.

YOUTHFUL GAMBLE

Q: Is the gambling sometimes managed or controlled by a state government or one of its agencies?

A: Yes.

Q: Are certain young adults not only permitted but also required to gamble?

A: Yes.

Q: Can the gambling be repeated by putting one's winnings at financial risk?

A: No.

Q: Could the skit be rewritten so that the roulette bet was concealed from the view of the audience, or removed entirely?
A: No.
Q: Could the roulette wheel be partially hidden?
A: No.
Q: Was gambling a significant problem in that town?
A: Yes.

NORTH, SOUTH, EAST, AND WEST

THE DEADLY SCULPTURE

He lived a lonely life in a remote building.

He made the statue out of copper. It was taken far away and he never saw it again.

He died as the result of an accident. No other person or animal or sculpture was involved.

PEAK PERFORMANCE

He had been dead for many years, so it was not possible to tell from his physical condition or clothing whether he had reached the summit.

The manner of his death is not relevant.

No camera was involved.

What would he have done had he reached the summit?

THE FATAL FISH

The man died in an accident. He was not poisoned or stabbed.

No other person was involved. No crime was involved.

The man did not eat the fish. The type of fish is irrelevant. It was dead.

He was not indoors.

ADAM HAD NONE

It has nothing to do with family, relations, bones, or physical appearance.

It has to do with names.

SHOT DEAD

The woman and the strangers were neither criminals nor police.

The strangers did not see the woman and did not know that she was in the house.

The strangers were armed and were a threat to the woman.

WOULD YOU BELIEVE IT?

The blocks of wood were identical and so were the people (for the purposes of this puzzle), but their circumstances were not identical.

Normal forces were at work in all three cases—nothing unusual was going on.

JAILBREAK

There was an advantage to him in escaping in the

morning. It had nothing to do with light, or deliveries, or prison officer routines.

He did not want to be spotted once he was outside the prison.

He knew that his escape would be detected after about half an hour.

SITTING DUCKS

The woman loves animals and hates hunting. She does not intend to use the gun for hunting or for self-defense.

There is no criminal intent in mind.

The ducks are already dead when she shoots them.

BALD FACTS

Mary, Queen of Scots took great care never to be seen without her wig.

Her wig was very good and looked completely natural.

Although Mary, Queen of Scots never wanted to be seen without her wig, she was not upset or embarrassed when it eventually happened, even though many people saw it.

LETHAL ACTION

The dead people were Africans. They didn't eat the fruit.

The Brazilian authorities' actions involved pesticides.

The Africans acted illegally. Their deaths were accidents.

RECOGNITION

His Aunt Mary was not carrying a sign or wearing anything distinctive. She did not have any disabilities or characteristics that would make her stand out.

He had not arranged to meet her in a specific place or

asked her to wear or carry anything in particular.

He recognized her from her facial appearance.

DESTRUCTION

The customer was a man who accidentally destroyed the premises without knowing that he was doing so.

He was there the whole time that the premises were being destroyed.

He was very overweight.

WONDERFUL WALK

Something annoying happened during the walk in the woods.

It gave the man an idea.

He invented a popular fastener.

PESKY ESCALATOR

There was no one else around.

The foreign visitor saw a sign.

He was very obedient.

POLES APART

The explorers knew that there would be no sources of food other than what they carried with them.

They did something that would not normally be considered a good idea.

ARRESTED DEVELOPMENT

The robber wanted to get out of the bank as quickly as he could.

There was nothing particularly noticeable or remarkable about the bank robber that would make him easy to identify.

He was not very bright.

HOLED OUT

It was not a good shot that got him the hole in one.

He should have been more careful.

The golfer's ball rebounded into the hole.

Another person was involved.

TRUNK-ATED

The policeman is able to prove that there is something suspicious in the trunk without opening it.

He suspects that there is a body in the trunk.

How do you attempt to contact a dead man?

SPORTS MAD

The sports fan was not exercising. He was not injured. He wanted the tape because of his sports obsession.

No sports equipment is involved.

He was a football fan. He followed his team fanatically but rarely got the chance to go to the games.

APPENDECTOMY I & II

No financial gain is involved in either solution.

The doctors who remove the healthy appendixes acted out of good motives.

Both solutions involve situations in the first part of the 20th century.

Riotous Assembly

The section did not have the equipment it needed to reopen.

The rioters had used everything they could lay their hands on.

The police had intervened but were driven back when the rioters threw rocks at them.

Kneed to Know

The man and his wife were in a room full of people.

She put her hand on his knee not as a sign of affection or encouragement but as an act of communication.

He gained an understanding through her actions.

Bad Trip

The anti-drug agency wanted to actively promote a message that drugs were bad, but inadvertently they ended up promoting the opposite message.

The agency distributed pencils to children and the children used them.

Two Letters

He is not trying to form words or to communicate or send a message.

The man is working on a crossword puzzle.

The letters he writes are S and E.

Body of Evidence

The woman was seen entering and leaving the police station, but no one tried to stop her.

She was not a criminal or deliberately aiding a criminal. She was doing her job.

SHAKESPEARE'S BLUNDER

The blunder did not involve physics, chemistry, mathematics, or astronomy.

The blunder concerned the twins, Viola and Sebastian.

NO CHARGE

The arresting officer followed the correct procedure and read the man his rights. There was clear evidence of his crime. But his lawyer got him released on a clear breach of his rights.

The crime he committed is irrelevant.

He did not own any music CDs or radios.

POND LIFE

The same environmental change would have occurred if felt hats or woolen hats had become very popular.

More silk hats were sold and fewer other hats were sold.

Fur hats were out of fashion.

SHOE SHOP SHUFFLE

The four shops have similar staffing, lighting, and security arrangements.

The shop that suffers the heaviest thefts is not in a worse part of town or in an environment that is more popular with criminals.

The shop that suffers the heaviest thefts does something different with its shoes.

CAESAR'S BLUNDER

The sea was calm and there were no storms when Caesar sailed across the channel and arrived in Britain.

He arrived safely and disembarked his troops and equipment.

Caesar had never visited Britain before.

He had learned to sail in the Mediterranean.

SLOW DEATH

Aeschylus did not trip over the tortoise or slip on it.

He did not eat it or attempt to eat it. He was not poisoned or bitten by the tortoise.

No other human was involved in his death.

DRIVING AWAY

Driving conditions were excellent, but the thief found the woman's car very difficult to drive.

She had had the car modified.

The rich woman suffered from some of the same frailties as other old people.

There was nothing unusual about the car's engine, gears, wheels, steering, or bodywork.

LIT TOO WELL?

The authorities deliberately set up lights in fields and on roads even though people living there had not requested them and did not need them.

There was damage to fields, crops, roads, and farm animals as a result.

Overall, though, human lives were saved.

QUICK ON THE DRAW

He had a perfectly valid ticket for that day's lottery, but he was not a prizewinner.

He saw the exact numbers on his ticket come up on the TV show.

He had a cruel wife.

SCALED DOWN

The butcher had only one turkey left.

He weighed it for the customer.

He pressed down on the scale with his thumb in order to give it an exaggerated weight.

THE HAPPY WOMAN

Although she used a driver, she walked about four miles in the course of her tour.

She wore special shoes.

She saw many flags.

VANDAL SCANDAL

The authorities did not add extra security or protection for the ancient buildings.

They fooled the people who were determined to take souvenirs.

Tourists went away happy.

THE DEADLY DRAWING

She was correct in her deduction that someone had been killed.

She did not know the person who had been killed, nor

who had killed them, nor how they had died.

She had never been in that room before and she had not seen the picture before.

Leonardo's Secret

Leonardo hid the designs in a place where he thought nobody would ever find them, but they were not buried or locked away.

People carefully stored the hidden designs for years without realizing they had them.

Down Periscope

The submarine was in water at all times and was not on dry ground or in dry dock.

No water entered the submarine.

This could happen only in certain places, and not in the open sea.

The Letter Left Out

The letter that is left out is chosen not because it is rarely used but because it is easily substituted without any risk of misunderstanding.

Arrested Development—Again

The robbers wore masks so as not to be recognized.
They made a clean getaway.
Bank employees noticed something about the two men.
The men were brothers.

Titanic Proportions

The ship that sank was not involved in the sinking of

the Titanic or the rescue operation.

Laws were passed to ensure that ships improved their safety.

One ship sank but all the passengers were saved.

THE MOVER

It is something you see every day.

In fact you have seen one in the last few seconds.

DEATH OF A PLAYER

The man was not involved in any collisions or tackles and did not suffer any injuries, yet it was because of his sport that he accidentally died.

He was a golfer, but he was not hit by a club or a ball or indeed by anything.

If only he had put his tee in his pocket!

HOT PICTURE

She loved the picture, but she deliberately had it burned. No trace of it was left.

There was no criminal intent on her part, and she did not make any financial gains.

The picture was a present.

Her husband was a motorcyclist.

GENUINE ARTICLE

The play was written by Shakespeare and this was proven beyond doubt.

It had been copied and written out on a computer, so there were no clues from the paper or handwriting.

No analysis of the style or content was needed to prove its authenticity.

Unhealthy Lifestyle

The man's unhealthy habits helped save him.
No other people were involved.
The woman died from poison.

New World Record

She did not do anything physical.
She became the only known person to achieve a certain feat.
It was not her age alone that did this, though one would have to be old to do it.

Death by Romance

They did not die of food or gas poisoning, nor from the effects of any kind of exertion.
They were not murdered. They died by accident.
They were in an unusual house.

Penalty

It was a regular soccer match played in the World Cup in front of thousands of people.
The players were not criminals or terrorists—just soccer players.
The match was played in an Arab country.

Golf Challenge I, II & III

I. The woman's gender was no handicap.
II. The woman was more than a match for the man.
III. It was a very wet day and the golf course was flooded.

Poor Investment

There were no other buildings nearby, and no buildings or roads were added or removed in the vicinity.

There were no earthquakes, floods, fires, or eruptions, and no damage by trees or vegetation.

The house had a beautiful view.

Give Us a Hand . . .

The man whose hand it was had also been looking for precious stones.

He had been forced to cut off his own hand.

To find these precious stones, men needed strong limbs, good eyes, good lungs, and great fitness.

Evil Intent

It was nothing she said or did with the man. He did not remember anything to cause his realization that she planned to burgle him.

He noticed something.

While he was preparing the drinks, she did something.

He had his hands full.

Two Heads Are Better Than One!

They were not drunk or under any strange influence.

This happened in North America.

They had seen a creature they had never seen before.

Stone Me!

The man was much bigger than the boy.

The stone hit the man on the head.

Many people watched.

Judge for Yourself

The defendant's actions probably influenced the judge in his favor.

The judge was scrupulously honest and would resent any intent to bribe or influence him.

Love Letters

She didn't know the men and didn't like any of them.

She had malicious intentions.

There was potential financial gain for her.

Strange Behavior

There were many trees along the side of the road. The man had never seen or noticed this tree before.

There was something different about this tree.

His primary concern was safety.

The tree itself was not a threat to him.

Tree Trouble

The wall was successful in keeping prying people away from the tree—just as intended.

The tree died.

The Burial Chamber

The burial chamber wasn't built for use by the builder.

He wrecked it before anyone was buried there.

He did not wreck it out of spite or anger. He deliberately destroyed it in order to deceive.

He wrecked the chamber in order to save the chamber.

MISCARRIAGE OF JUSTICE

The Italian judge tried a rebel, but released a robber.

The Italian was not in Italy when he made the judgment.

The judge, the rebel, and the robber never ate any chocolate.

OFFENSES DOWN

The police officers filled in their reports and forms in a different fashion, which reduced crime, but they did not fill them in any better or quicker or more accurately or with more information than before.

They filled in the reports by hand, not by computer.

The key difference was their location when they did the paperwork.

POLICE CHASE

The fast police car was right behind the criminals' vehicle and there was no other traffic or vehicle involved. The roads were clear and the weather was fine.

The getaway vehicle was a bus.

The bus driver was number seven.

CAFÉ SOCIETY

The café owner did not change the menu or prices or music in the café.

He changed the appearance of the café in a way that embarrassed the teenagers.

Hi, Jean!

The shop owner sold food and he wanted to present it in the best possible light.

He took action to deter and kill pests.

The Empty Machine

Kids had cheated the gum company.

They had not put quarters into the machine, but they had obtained gumballs.

The machine was rusty, but it still worked fine.

Take a Fence

No other person or animal was involved.

The change in color was not caused by the sun or wind.

The change in color was caused by the rain, but every other house and fence in the area remained unchanged in color.

Sex Discrimination

The prison guards were not acting in a discriminatory, sexist, or unfair fashion, but simply following procedures.

Women were more likely to fall afoul of the security equipment.

Weight Loss

The diet and the daily regimen were not changed. But something else about the clinic was changed, and this produced the weight loss in patients.

The change made the patients work a little harder in normal activities.

The fact that the clinic is in Japan is not particularly relevant. Similar results could have been obtained in many countries—but not in Belgium or Holland.

Psychic

You see the cars after you see the woman, and you did not see her leaving the car.

There is something different in the appearance of her car.

She is carrying something.

The Happy Robber

He was poor. He stole something from the bank, but it was not money.

He made no financial gain from the theft. He stole for love.

He stole a rare liquid.

Siege Mentality

This took place in the Middle Ages.

The defenders had plenty of food, water, and ammunition.

The attackers had catapulted rocks over the walls, but had now run out of ammunition.

Carrier Bags

The suggestion was a way of creating new aircraft carriers much more cheaply than by the conventional methods.

It would possibly have been practical in the North Atlantic.

They were disposable carriers.

The Cathedral Untouched

The area all around St. Paul's was heavily bombed, but it appeared that no bombs could fall on St. Paul's.

The German bombers deliberately avoided bombing it.

They were not acting out of any religious or moral principles.

Bags Away

The passenger's suitcase was stored in the hold of the plane.

He was not a terrorist or criminal.

The passenger's suitcase did not contain chemicals, explosives, or drugs.

The Sad Samaritan

Jim was not robbed or deceived by the motorist in any way.

Jim tried his best to help, but failed.

The motorist was stranded.

The Tallest Tree

The men did not use angles or shadows.

They did not climb the tree.

They measured it accurately using rope and measuring lines.

The Unwelcome Guest

The neighbor liked the dog and the dog did not annoy the neighbor.

The couple gave the neighbor a fine meal.

He was horrified at what happened next.

POOR SHOW

His performances were always a flop, but he was very successful.

He was not in comedy, music, cinema, or theater.

His most famous performance was in Mexico.

He was a sportsman.

MESSAGE RECEIVED

Envoys were thoroughly searched when they arrived at a foreign location to check for hidden messages.

The envoys did not memorize the messages or ever know or see the contents of the messages.

The messages were hidden on the person of the envoy but they could not be seen, even when the envoy was naked.

THE MIGHTY STONE

The peasant did not suggest building over it.

He suggested a way of moving the stone, but not by pushing it or pulling it.

He used its own weight to help move it.

THE WORLD'S MOST EXPENSIVE CAR

The car was used once and is in good condition, but it has not been driven for many years.

Most people have seen it on TV, but they can't name the man who drove it.

It is not associated with any celebrity or with any remarkable historical event or tragedy, though when it was driven it was a special event at the time.

It was developed at great expense for practical use and not for show or exhibition.

The Fatal Fall

The woman wasn't a criminal, and no crime was involved.

She was quite upset to have dropped the piece of wood.

The wood was a cylinder about one foot long.

The piece of wood was not particularly valuable and could easily be replaced.

Many people saw her drop the piece of wood.

Election Selection

The successful candidate had no particular experience, qualifications, or characteristics that qualified him for the job or increased his appeal to voters.

He did not canvass or advertise or spend money in any way to influence the voters, and he remained unknown to the voters.

The other candidates were competent and trustworthy and did nothing to disqualify themselves.

He changed something about himself.

Well Trained

Do not take this puzzle too seriously—it involves a bad pun.

The child was correct. But why?

Razor Attack

She meant to hurt him, and he did not defend himself.

The razor made full contact with his unprotected throat.

She could not have shaved him either.

The Old Crooner

Bing Crosby himself did not take part in the action to reduce crime.

His songs were used to reduce crime.

His songs are old-fashioned and melodic, which means that some people like them and some do not.

The Parson's Pup

The fact that he is religious is not relevant.

The vicar is particular about his appearance.

Generosity?

He had not intended to give any money away, and did not do so out of altruistic motives.

He was under pressure.

Watch That Man!

The wristwatch was perfectly legal and did not give the runner an unfair advantage.

The man had cheated.

The clue to his cheating was that his wristwatch had changed hands.

TRICKY

The Tracks of My Tires

The police didn't ask any questions but merely used their powers of observation.

When the police arrived, none of the three suspects was

carrying a weapon or wearing blood-stained clothing.

The police correctly deduced that the woman was the murderer.

THE UPSET WOMAN

He was an unwelcome intruder.
He had visited before, so she left some food for him.
She wanted him to die.

BERTHA'S TRAVELS

Bertha is a woman who normally travels with other people.
She doesn't travel by walking or running, nor by plane or boat.
She provides a service to passengers.

SICK LEAVE

Walter was human and physically normal.
The hospital was a normal hospital.
He wasn't able to walk into the hospital or out of it.

TOP AT LAST

William didn't cheat.
He didn't revise or work any harder than usual.
He wasn't particularly happy to be top of the list.

CRIMINAL ASSISTANCE

The police notices were to warn people about certain types of thieves.
The thieves observed people's reactions to the signs.

In the Middle of the Night

He didn't hear or smell anything that might have helped him.

The watch wasn't luminous.

None of the objects could be seen in the pitch dark.

Honorable Intent

The six people had never met the seventh person and never would meet him.

The seventh person wasn't famous, remarkable, or well known.

The six people all owed a great debt to the seventh person—but not a financial debt.

Shell Shock

The game is rigged.

The dealer is fast, but it isn't speed alone that deceives the player.

Wonderful Weather

The accident happened at night.

Material Witness

They are perfectly normal curtains and not special.

Denise and Harry

Denise and Harry harmed people.

They weren't humans but they weren't animals either.

MECHANICAL ADVANTAGE

The problem wasn't with the engine of his car.

It was raining.

He bought something sweet and used that to solve the problem.

LIFESAVER

Any speech of the same length would have had the same effect.

Someone made an attempt on his life.

UNFINISHED BUSINESS

The work isn't necessarily big.

Many people undertake this work.

None of them can ever truly complete it.

THE DEADLY DRESSER

If he had not dressed, he would not have died.

He died by accident.

He was poisoned.

LANDLUBBER

He circumnavigated the world and crossed every line of longitude.

There was nothing special about his boat or on his boat.

He sailed his boat around the world but always stayed within a few miles of shore.

He did it from November to February.

Another Landlubber

He went around quite quickly.

He saw Africa, Asia, Europe, North America, and South America.

He didn't sail the ship.

Plane and Simple

The tree was normal and the boy was normal.

Trees grow differently from boys.

Jericho

Although he constructed it with great care, the man thought that the house might fall down.

He didn't intend that he or anyone else live in the house.

Superior Knowledge

Nobody said anything, but there was visible evidence of the man's presence.

It was nothing to do with shaving.

Half for Me and Half for You

Lucrezia Borgia's companion died of poisoning.

The apple was taken at random from a bowl of perfectly good apples.

Lucrezia deliberately killed her companion.

Rush Job

He exploited a different need of the miners.

He turned the tents to some other use—not accommodation.

The tents were made of heavy denim material.

THE ENGRAVING

What she received wasn't what she expected.
A fine artist had created the picture she received.
The engraving had already been put to use.

WHO DID IT?

The teacher didn't threaten or bribe any child.
No child admitted the misdemeanor or tattled on anyone else.
The teacher gave the class an exercise to do.

LETHAL RELIEF

They didn't die of hunger, disease, or food poisoning.
The relief was delivered to remote areas.
The people died before they opened the packages of food.

HOT JOB

The robber's face was covered, but he was easily identified.
His choice of clothing was poor.

CHOP CHOP

The tree was not hazardous, harmful, or threatening in any way.
The problem does not involve animals, students, seeds, leaves, roots, or branches.
The problem related to the tree's location.

RESISTANCE

The booby traps depended on a likely action that Germans might take.

Germans have a reputation for being well organized, neat, and tidy.

BASKET CASE

She was very well known in her time.
She was involved in the execution of people.
She never said a word.

INVISIBLE EARNINGS

Nauru exports something of value.
It has nothing to do with tourism, finance, or crafts.
There are many seabirds in Nauru.

ABSOLUTE MADNESS

They were received into the hospital as insane.
They had not carried out any action to indicate that they were insane.
They hadn't met before, but there was a link between them.
They had all set out to travel by bus.

SPIES ARE US

They went to the restaurant as paying customers.
No codes were used, and they never spoke or sat near each other.
They dressed in similar clothes.

TITTLE TATTLE

Tittles are seen in print.
There are two in this sentence.

OUTSTANDING

The feature of The Old Farmer's Almanac that made it
more popular had nothing to do with its printed contents.
It had no value other than as an almanac.
Its advantage was practical.

THE STUFFED CLOUD

The meteorologist died.
He wasn't aware of the stuffed cloud. It hadn't affected
any of his forecasts or reports.
He was traveling.

A STRANGE COLLECTION

The contents are inedible, but they are not bones or
animal parts.
They had done something relevant together earlier in
the day.
They are eating game.

FOREIGN CURE

He didn't go abroad for drugs, medicines, treatments,
or cures that were unavailable in the U.S.
His illness was curable given the right motivation.
He went to an Arab country.

Bus Lane Bonus

The bus lanes were introduced because of heavy traffic congestion. Normal traffic was forbidden to use the bus lanes so the buses could move more quickly.

The reduction in death rate wasn't due to fewer road accidents, fewer pedestrian accidents, less pollution, or fewer cars in the city.

Accident victims were saved.

Blow by Blow

He was secretly blowing darts at particular targets.

His nefarious actions generated more sales at the fairground.

History Question

September 8, 1752, was a very unusual day—but there were 10 other days like it.

No significant wars, births, deaths, disasters, achievements, or discoveries happened in London that day.

Sign Here

He had intended to use the two signs in two places to give the same message, but he found that that didn't work.

He was advertising his roadside café.

Paper Tiger

The sheets of paper were important. He wrote the numbers in ink.

He intended to keep the papers for his later personal use. He did this each year at a certain time of year.

Forging Ahead

He used the $50 bill to help pass a forged bill—but not a forged $50 bill.

He bought something he didn't want.

Smile Please!

The toothpaste company adopted his idea and their sales increased.

It had nothing to do with the taste, price, or distribution of the toothpaste.

The idea encouraged people to use more toothpaste.

High on a Hill

The man managed to stay warm but he didn't burn anything.

The man was alone. No person or animal helped him to keep warm.

The mountain was dangerous.

Mine Shafted

The buyer explored the mine and found the silver as was intended.

They were genuine pieces of silver but not the sort you would find in a silver mine.

That Will Teach You

This didn't happen at night.

He hadn't left any heating, lighting, or cooking equipment on.

The thing he had forgotten had helped cause a fire.

A Geography Question

Three of the answers are routine, but one is unexpected—and lateral!

Maine isn't the most eastern state.

The Generous General

The general felt he had been misled.

The recipient's response wasn't what the general expected.

Fast Mover!

The man didn't use airplanes or super-fast ground transport.

He did not need his passport.

Running on Empty

Something bad was averted.

Nobody was driving the car when it ran out of gas.

What's the Point?

A round pencil would not do.

She hates losing pencils.

The Office Job

The man's age, appearance, gender, and dress didn't matter.

Everyone had completed the form correctly and in a similar fashion.

The man showed that he had a skill required for the job.

HEARTY APPETITE

The whale was a killer whale.
The whale was at sea.
The people who were disappointed hadn't come to see the whale.

THE UPSET BIRD WATCHER

The bird was just as beautiful and rare as he had imagined. He wasn't disappointed with its appearance.
What happened to the bird placed him at risk.
He saw the bird through a small window.

FLOATING HOME

The man was normal, but he had been on an extraordinary voyage.
He had not set off by sea, but he had always intended to return in the manner in which he did.
He returned safe and well. He was found by people who were concerned for his well-being.

CO-LATERAL DAMAGE

Some damage is fatal to a plane and some is not.
The returning planes are not a true sample of all the planes and all the damage.
U.S. bomber command used the information about damage on returning planes to strengthen planes and so reduce losses.

ORSON CART

The group that wasn't fooled did not know the plot of

the play or the book, nor did they spot any production flaw.

They were children.

THROWING HIS WEIGHT ABOUT

The man was normal, fit, and healthy.
He died by accident.
He was trying to demonstrate something.

DISCONNECTED?

The horse was alive throughout and was not exceptional.
The horse was a working horse.
The two legs that traveled farthest were the front left and back left.

JOKER

They weren't playing strip poker and stripping wasn't a forfeit or penalty involved in the game.
The actual card game isn't relevant.
She took off her clothes to avoid harm.

Rich Man, Poor Man

It has nothing to do with the costs or prices of tea or milk.

It has nothing to do with the taste or flavor of the tea.

It concerns the cups from which they drank their tea.

Mined Over Matter

The mine was live and dangerous. It would explode if it came into contact with metal.

He took some action to deflect the mine from the ship.

He did not touch or defuse the mine.

Surprise Visit

The factory manager and his staff cleared away all the rubbish and left the factory looking spotlessly clean.

The chairman arrived in an unexpected fashion.

He saw a terrible mess.

School's Out

She was instructed to go to school for her education.

She was already very old (and well educated).

She was issued the court order automatically.

The Deadly Stone

The blood on the stone was the man's blood. It had been put there two days before his death.

Nobody else was involved.

He had marked the stone with his blood for a purpose.

THE COSTLY WAVE

He wasn't at an auction.
He waved to fans and onlookers.

2020 VISION

The farmer was being truthful.
Exactly 22 pigs were stolen.

THE DEADLY OMELET

He was a wanted man.
The omelet and its ingredients were relevant.
He had not done anything illegal.
This incident happened in France.

THE GAP

He was writing in an unusual way.
The writing was important and would be seen by many people.
He was planning ahead.

THE DINNER CLUE

The police obtained the evidence they needed.
He didn't finish his meal.

WRONG WAY

The man had a rational reason for choosing a bus going in the opposite direction to the one he wanted.
His reason was not to do with saving money, saving time, avoiding danger, seeing anything, or meeting anyone.
His reason has to do with comfort.

The Single Word

Other people also heard what she had to say.

There is no sexual connotation to this story. The narrator could be male or female.

The word I said summarized a decision that would significantly affect the woman.

None of my companions was allowed to speak in the woman's presence.

The Man Who Would Not Read

Conditions on the train were perfectly suitable for reading.

He was very obedient.

No local resident would have made the same mistake.

Not Eating?

The hungry man wanted to eat and there was no medical, religious, or financial reason for him not to eat.

He was physically fit, healthy, and normal.

He was in the same room as his plate and the plate had food on it. But he wasn't able to eat it.

Two Pigs

They were sold on the same day at the same market.

Each was sold for a fair price.

The two pigs looked the same, but when they were sold one was worth much more than the other.

One was sold for food—the other was not.

Eensy Weensy Spider Farm

It was relevant that the spider farms were in France.
The spiderwebs were used, but not to catch anything.
They are found in wine-growing regions.

Face-off

The soldiers were killed, but not in action, nor by disease, flood, storm, or fire.
It was during winter.
Some test shots were fired, but the shells fell well away from the soldiers.

Cheap and Cheerful

The fresh food was in perfectly good condition.
The man was normal and didn't have any allergies or aversions.
The food was salmon.

Up in Smoke

The cigars were valuable. He didn't steal or sell them.
He was perfectly entitled to smoke them.
He successfully claimed the $10,000, and as a result was found guilty of a crime.

Silly Cone

The office manager found a way to make people waste less time.
The cones were given away free.
A cone will not rest on its end.

Not the Führer

There were no identity tags or personal effects that would have revealed the man's identity.

There were no distinguishing marks on the man's body.

His clothing gave the clue.

Vase and Means

They discovered the ingredient by accident.

The ingredient strengthened the pottery.

The accident was a tragedy.

My Condiments to the Chef

The owner wasn't trying to save money or be more efficient.

There had been a problem involving the bottles of vinegar.

He was trying to discourage a certain group of customers.

The Man Who Did Not Fly

The fictitious person did not exist and did not fly.

The police knew about this situation.

Other passengers had been victims of a crime.

Inheritance

Both sons reached the shore. The younger was judged to have touched the shore first.

The younger son took drastic action.

Stamp Dearth Death

If he had bought the right postage, he would have lived.
He sent a package.

Rock of Ages

He was oblivious to all around him.
He was struck with a strong blow.
His wife tried to help him.

Quo Vadis?

The archaeologist didn't use any written or pictorial evidence.
He deduced that Romans drove their chariots on the left-hand side of the road from physical evidence. But not from the remains of chariots.
He excavated a Roman quarry.

Pork Puzzler

The bacon served a purpose on the journey but was never used as food.
He packed it at the top of his suitcase.
Bacon is offensive to certain people.

Frozen Assets

The railway was needed temporarily to carry cargo to a certain location.
It was possible to lay tracks over the land to reach the place, but they were unable to do so.
They wanted to supply food and ammunition.

Turned Off

The man didn't interfere with the physical operation of the radio stations.

There was no threat or misinformation.

All radio stations voluntarily chose to stop transmitting for a short period.

The Last Mail

There was no difference in the contents, envelope, or addressing of the two letters.

They were both sent by the same method—first class.

The same clerk at the same post office handled both letters.

The man weighed the letters and found their weights were identical. He then put stamps on them and took them to the postal clerk, who told him that one of the letters was fine but that the other needed more stamps.

Small Is Not Beautiful

It doesn't have to do with pollution, crime, economy, car production, or politics.

The reason concerned safety.

Small cars were more dangerous in certain types of accidents that occur often in Sweden.

The Deadly Feather

The man was physically fit and healthy.

The feather had touched him.

He was a circus performer.

The Sealed Room

Nothing else and nobody else was involved except the man and the sealed room.

He died slowly but not from lack of food, water, or oxygen. If he had not been in the sealed room, he would have lived.

Written Down

She is writing in an unusual place.

She has difficulty writing the letters P, R, T, and Z but no difficulty with O, Q, S, U, X, and Y.

She is writing on thick books.

Publicity Puzzler

The two men both share a problem. It's an unusual problem. It's not identical for each man.

By shopping together they gain a financial benefit.

They shop for one type of item only. It's not food, furniture, or electrical goods.

Who Wants It Anyway?

It's something that can be won or lost. If you lose it, then you suffer financial and other penalties.

No other craft was involved.

The accident happened in winter.

Knights of Old

It doesn't concern horses or weapons.

The custom has evolved and is used today by military personnel for a different purpose.

Originally it involved sight and recognition.

Shave That Pig!

The pigs were used for something other than food.
This happened only in winter.

Watch Out!

The man thought it was much later than it actually was.
It was dark when he went outside.
The man was unusual.

The Wedding Present

He was embarrassed with shame when his gift was opened.

His gift wasn't offensive to the bride and groom in any religious, political, or moral way.

He had bought an expensive gift but then made a mistake and tried to save money.

Murder Mystery

Both the husband and wife had been married before.

Their marriage was successful and neither was unfaithful to the other.

She killed her husband to help someone she loved.

SOLUTIONS

Welcome, Slasher

A hurricane emergency had been declared, and poorly construct-ed buildings were at risk of major structural damage. Screens imposed wind resistance which could stress buildings enough to wreck them. Removing screens from screened porches was cor-rectly announced as a safety measure, even if the screens were per-manently stapled in place, so the boy had an opportunity to divert his destructive tendencies to a good cause. The policeman knew that the frantic absent homeowners had requested the boy's help with this potential problem.

Smashed Taillights

Bob had been kidnapped and locked in a car trunk. Aware of police department recommendations, he fumbled for the tire wrench and, having loosened it from its storage brackets, broke the taillights and side markers from inside. Then he was able to wave the wrench to passers-by and to call for help.

Supposed to Kill?

A scene was being filmed for a movie. For the protection of actors, it was universally agreed that anyone on the receiving end of a firearm had to load it personally with nonhazardous "blanks." This particular actor had forgotten to load the gun, and the scene had to be refilmed.

Burning Down the Building

The landlord set fire to his own building. It was occupied by tenants who paid a low rent that was restricted by law. If they moved out, then he would have vacant apartments that could be offered at a much higher rent than before. Incurring fire damage was a sensible investment, for it would remove the low-rent tenants and permit elegant remodeling into luxury apartments that could fetch a very high rent.

Caught in the Act

In this true story, a neighborhood pickpocket was caught by a woman, the wife of eighteenth-century inventor Peter Cooper, who sewed fishhooks into her coat pocket. When he caught his hand on the hooks, she told him, "I am going to the police station, and you are coming with me." He cooperated to prevent serious injury to his hand.

Slippery Sidney Slipped Up

Sidney was arrested for turning back the odometer and understating the number of miles that he actually drove. While at a distant city, he received two parking tickets from two different officers and didn't pay them. The city charged the fines to the rental-car company, and the company inferred that Sidney had driven the car there. But Sidney had not put enough mileage on the car, according to the odometer, to have been able to do so. The evidence was strong enough to convict him.

HONEST IVAN

Noting the much lower per-day cost of renting a car in Florida than in Washington, Ivan rented the car in Florida. He had it shipped from central Florida to a town in northern Virginia, where he retrieved it. The shipping cost was less than the total savings from renting the car in Florida and returning it to where he got it. By proving that he had sent the car by train, he convinced investigators that the odometer reading was genuine.

ROBBING THE BANK

The organization was the local police force, and the numerous officers who were standing in line to cash their paychecks easily captured all of the would-be robbers.

HE CALLED THE POLICE

Once inside the house, he fell, breaking his leg. Pulling a telephone down from a table, he called an emergency police number for help and, though arrested, received treatment for his leg.

ARRESTED ANYWAY

Rocky took one airplane to an intermediate stop, got out, and got into a second airplane to his final destination. If he had told the airline that he was doing so, then his fare would have been higher. He was trying to save money by noting that the fares for the separate parts of his trip were less than the equivalent fare for the whole trip. Therefore, he could not check the suitcase directly to the final destination, but had to retrieve it and re-check it at the intermediate stop. Rocky did not have a firearm permit for the state in which he made the intermediate stop, but was carrying the gun. He was arrested for that reason.

No Ransom Demand

The man was a cancer patient and was getting weaker and weaker. He had no medical insurance and would soon need hospital care. Confined to a wheelchair, he sat on the gun as he entered the government building. He threatened people in a room next to the district attorney's office so that he would be apprehended as quickly as possible, and he happily went to prison. He knew that, while he was a prisoner, the government would pay his medical expenses and that life as a hospital patient is essentially identical with or without serving a prison sentence.

Escaping the Kidnappers

A dial rapidly breaks and reconnects the telephone circuit. When you dial a number, you make the dial spin at a controlled rate and temporarily break the circuit that number of times when the dial is released. Without access to the dial, Brenda placed her fingers on the telephone switch-hook (where the handset is placed when the phone is hung up) and removed them rapidly exactly ten times, dialing "0" so as to reach the operator. The operator quickly connected her to the police department.

Hearing Them Quickly

The father had noticed the planned live concert and noticed that it was also to be on television. Microphones would be a few feet from the performers and would capture the sound for television transmission. The audience, potentially including Dana, would be farther from the performers than the microphones would be. Sound travels at about 800 feet per second. Television waves and the electric currents that create and respond to them travel over a million times faster than sound. The father correctly figured that the television audience would hear the performance sooner than the live audience, for there would be less delay while sound waves travel the short distance to the microphones and from TV speakers to viewers than while sound waves travel the full distance from performers to the live audience. The difference is only a fraction of a second, but the father was nevertheless telling the truth.

MOTORCYCLE MADNESS

Amy knew that the official penalty for trespassing was merely a small fine. She reasoned that, unable to identify Peter or know whether or not he was armed, the motorcyclists might count themselves lucky to have escaped apparent great danger and would spread the word that that piece of land was unfriendly, thereby encouraging others to stay away.

A CRYING PROBLEM

After she and her husband had a particularly nasty argument, he had stormed out. She suspected that, as he had done previously, he had returned to his parents. Therefore, she called them hoping that they would tell her where he was. When they did not, she became very upset.

SHE NEVER FIXED HIM UP

Mitch and Anna got married and lived happily ever after.

HAPPY THAT SHE CURSED HIM

She was married to another man, and he suggested that she pretend that he was an obnoxious telephone solicitor if he called while her husband might overhear. His ruse apparently worked, and he was pleased.

EVICTED

The son, in his late teens, was spoiled and idle. The father correctly inferred that evicting him and forcing him to earn his own way would benefit him, however unpleasant it would be at first. When the son found a job and had worked at it for a while, he understood how his father's action had made his life more respectable and constructive. Therefore, he thanked his father.

DRIVING THE WRONG CAR

The battery on the broken car was dead, and Hermie knew that the electrical system was suspect. He wanted the car checked thoroughly. He jump-started it with the working car, after which it could be driven. The working car had a manual transmission and could be towed without transmission damage. But the jump-started car had an automatic transmission, which is affected by towing. Hermie, therefore, towed the car that had the manual transmission.

SAFE SMASH-UP

No one was in the car. It had been parked on a hill, and the driver who parked it forgot to set the brakes. Since the ignition was not on, there was no spark or other flame source to set fire to the fuel.

CONTAGIOUS CARSICKNESS?

Stan had, as he had planned, stopped the car on a ferry boat. Jan became seasick.

WHAT DRAINED THE BATTERY?

Walter, in a rush, forgot to turn off the headlights. No one else entered the parking lot until lunchtime, when managers customarily went out to eat. One of them turned off Walter's headlights, although by then the battery didn't have enough power to start the engine.

SEASONAL MILEAGE

Claude uses the air conditioner during summer. Just before the end of a trip, he turns it off so as not to waste fuel. He does not want to pay to keep the car cool while he is not in it. He is sensitive to cold, however; and he keeps the heat on whenever he needs it in winter, including when he is just about to get out of his car.

She Arrived On Time

Carol was not at home. She had had her telephone calls diverted to her cellular phone and simply happened to be in the coffeehouse when Daryl called her.

A Token Wait in a Token Line

Smart Stephanie observed that most commuters bought tokens as they entered the subway from the street. She merely bought tokens as she left the subway, when few other commuters did so.

The Late Train

During the night, which was the last Saturday in March, the time was advanced from standard time to daylight saving time. The engineer gained fifteen minutes during the night, but the train was still late when Amanda got off it.

Stubborn Steve

Steve was going to use the paper in airmail letters to correspondents overseas. To save postage, he wanted paper as light as possible, even if it was expensive and occasionally jammed his printer.

Making the Grade

Nell could not hand in a postcard with her term paper because, although the paper was not due for another week, she had already handed it in. She was then free to write other term papers and study for exams in other courses.

Spaced-Out at the Computer

First solution: If you know the maximum number of spaces in a row, take the exponent of the next highest power of 2 and enter the command to replace two spaces with one space that number of times. (Example: seven spaces maximum. Next highest power of two is eight, which is $2\check{\ }2\check{\ }2$, so use the command three times.) Second solution: Choose two characters that are never adjacent in either order (in this example, &%). First command: replace each space with &%. Second command: replace each %& (reverse the order of the characters) with nothing (delete %&). Third command: replace each &% with space.

The Fast Elevator Trip

When the elevator arrived, other people crowded into it; and Bill critically watched them push buttons for several floors. Bill figured that the elevator would stop at the most floors at which it could stop. Therefore, noting that another elevator was approaching, he decided to get onto it instead; for he would share it with fewer passengers while it made far fewer intermediate stops on the way to his appointment. Avoiding the intermediate stops was worth the wait.

The Nonstop Elevator Trip

The floor was at the top of one range of floors served by one group of elevators. Jill instead used the adjacent group of elevators, going to the lowest floor served by them, which was one floor above her floor. Then, after her nonstop elevator ride, she merely walked down one flight of stairs.

Too Precise

In a politician's campaign office. They were volunteers for a candidate who believed in straightforward platforms instead of vague speeches.

Exceptionally Vague

It was a label attached to a key to the politician's other campaign office. Keys are best labeled cryptically or so as to mislead, so that they will be easily used legitimately but will be worthless to someone who should not have them. Jerry insisted that the key to the other office, which was at the river, be labeled "River Bank and Trust."

The Hostile Voter

Charlie heard an aggressive sales pitch about a candidate who supposedly believed in keeping government as unobtrusive as possible. The volunteer was engaged in a meddlesome act, that of telephoning voters at home. Because the candidate approved such intrusive actions, Charlie deduced that the candidate was not going to keep his word about an unobtrusive government and decided not to vote for him.

A Mystery Fax

Quietly interested in changing jobs, the executive arranged for a cooperative recruiter to try to fax him a blank sheet of paper when trying to reach him. If he could talk, then he announced himself over the fax signal. If not, he called the recruiter later when he could discreetly do so.

Another Mystery Fax

The executive, aware of how easy it is to communicate with outsiders for undesirable purposes, warned employees that calls would be monitored. A subordinate, aware of the difficulties of monitoring a fax message, bypassed the monitoring by faxing instead of speaking his personal messages.

Problems with Personnel

Raymond, who was in charge of research, had requested and expected to hire someone with a master's degree. The applicant, who had a doctorate, was rejected by the personnel department because he didn't have a master's degree even though the doctorate was, in Raymond's opinion, preferable.

More Problems with Personnel

The applicant had had a roommate who was transferred overseas and who had impeccable credentials, but he himself was less scrupulous. He applied for work and gave his former roommate's name, background, and references. He wrote to Raymond's colleague and asked about work; they had never met. When the colleague saw that her apparent friend was an impostor, she said so; and Raymond promptly fired him.

Dismaying Dizziness

The lamp was fluorescent, and the new wallpaper had closely spaced vertical stripes. Fluorescent bulbs do not glow steadily, but flash 120 times per second. When viewing vertical stripes in fluorescent light, the intermittent lighting can make the stripes seem to turn as you turn your head, when they really stay fastened to the wall. This inconsistency is disturbing and is what caused the dizziness. The simplest remedy is to use only daylight. A more practical solution is to replace the fluorescent lamp with an incandescent one.

Giving Wayne the Boot

Burglars had cut the neighbor's telephone wire and broken into his house. In self-defense, he barricaded himself into an upstairs room and successfully provoked Wayne to call the police.

Racing the Drawbridge

Clarence was navigating a boat, and the drawbridge was opened to let it pass.

Recycled Salt

Bread recipes customarily call for small amounts of salt. By vigorously kneading bread dough and working up a sweat, one can add previously eaten salt to the dough so that it will be eaten again.

Scared of Her Shadow?

She drives an old car, with taillight lenses that have not been cleaned from the inside for perhaps ten years. Sunlight shining on taillight lenses can make brake and turn signals nearly impossible to see, particularly with dirty lenses or the dim bulbs in very old cars. Hand signals, under those circumstances, are more easily seen. Florida law permits hand signals for sufficiently small cars, even if the taillights work.

Picture the Tourists

Sal's camera focused by measuring the distance to the object in front of it, which would be the window of the bus. Sal's pictures of objects outside the bus would, therefore, be badly out of focus. But autofocus does not work when the distance is very small. Sherman wanted Sal to sit close to the window, so that the camera would ignore it and focus for great distance and would take good pictures.

The Mirror

It is one of two mirrors, both made of special optical-grade glass to prevent eyestrain. The mirror that is not over the headboard is mounted, on a flexible bracket, near it. After adjusting the second mirror, one can lie on one's back and look in it and see the reflection from the first mirror. By looking through two mirrors, one sees an unreversed image. This arrangement is useful for someone with a bad back who wants to lie in bed and watch television, for one need not be propped up but can lie truly flat.

THE EMPTY WRAPPER

She had her two-year-old son with her. When her son got hungry, she got permission from a store manager to buy a sandwich at the delicatessen counter, give it to her son, and pay for it later at the checkout counter with the rest of her merchandise.

SECRET FUEL

Marvin's neighbor had recently bought an extravagant sports car and bragged about it constantly. Hoping to quiet him down, Marvin poured a gallon of fuel into its fuel tank every few nights. After the neighbor began to boast about his new car's outstanding mileage, Marvin knew that his plan would work: merely add fuel quietly, then stop and let the neighbor wonder why the mileage suddenly deteriorated just as the warranty expired.

FORGOT TO STOP?

The car ran off a bridge and fell into a lake, and Angus jumped out just as the car hit its surface.

SHORT-LIVED MESSAGES

Yolanda has an IBM-compatible computer and an Apple computer and wants to transmit data between them. With only one modem and little technical knowledge, she sends the data to herself through an on-line electronic-mail service with one computer and receives the data with the other computer.

More Short-Lived Writing

Erasing colored chalk from a blackboard. Yolanda is a teacher and sometimes draws diagrams on the blackboard using different colors of chalk. Erasing such diagrams leaves colored smudges on the blackboard. Yolanda discovered that scribbling over the colored smudges with white chalk and then erasing the scribbling helps to remove the colored smudges and, unlike wiping the blackboard with a wet rag, permits immediate re-use of it.

The Mail Is In!

Oscar knew the procedure for receiving a package by mail. You take the key from your mailbox, unlock the pod, and take the package from the pod. The key stays in the pod door. Only a mail carrier can remove a key from a pod door. When Oscar saw a pod without a key and remembered that the pod had had a key on the previous day, he knew that the mail carrier had delivered the day's mail.

Magazine Subscriptions

Postage for a first-class item with a reply-paid address must be paid by the recipient. City residents may hoard the cards in case of a garbage collectors' strike, perhaps believing that those who contribute to the garbage problem should help solve it at their own expense.

Soliciting in Seattle

In Seattle, one building houses the headquarters of several charity canvassing organizations. They send workers out to collect money, and those workers usually walk from the building when they start canvassing and return to it on foot when they are finished. Only one of the friends' two houses was within easy walking distance of that building.

It's a Dog's Life

They were at an animal shelter, which had a surplus of unwanted pets and had to kill those that it could not give to willing owners. Fred knew that people were often more willing to adopt a disfigured pet than an intact one. The injured puppy was likely to be taken by a loving family, but the healthy dog had no special claim for compassion and was too old to bond to its owners as strongly as do young puppies. Therefore, Fred expected the older dog to be humanely killed.

Not from the USA

Windsor, Canada, adjacent to Detroit, Michigan, is directly both south and east of parts of Michigan. It is north and west of other USA states.

Dots on the I's

A small I has one dot over it. A small I with a dot over it, therefore, actually has two dots, one above the other. Timmy took a pen and put two dots on his forehead, one over each eye.

Power Failure

Power failures occurred often. Horace, therefore, did not bother resetting clocks every time the power was restored. When the power failed during the night, the clocks had not been reset from the previous power failure and looked unchanged in the morning.

Afraid of the Country

Nicolai was afraid of silence. While on a farm during World War II, he was exposed to the sounds of livestock. Under normal circumstances, farm animals move around and make noise from time to time. But when scared, they do not. They could hear

German bomber airplanes when people could not—and became silent. Silence, to Nicolai, meant that an air raid was imminent and that he would have to hide in the basement. Despite many decades since the war, Nicolai never recovered from his fear.

LONG-LIFE BULBS

Modern incandescent bulbs have a coiled filament that glows as current is passed through it. A coil, however, radiates and absorbs magnetic impulses as the current through it is changed. It thereby not only resists changes in current (the electrical equivalent of inertia), but also shakes slightly as the voltage changes. The voltage changes with alternating current between +166 volts and –166 volts and back again 60 times per second, placing mechanical stress on the filament. Eric merely used direct current, so that the filaments would not be shaken by voltage changes and would last longer for that reason.

THEY HAD A BALL

The two men were not alone. Ted saw a teammate behind Ned and feared that if Ned missed the high ball, then the teammate might be hit by it. A throw directly to someone's body was different, for it would at least be deflected if it was missed. Ted aimed his high throw so that if Ned missed the ball, it would not hit anyone.

BALLPARK BEFUDDLEMENT

The nine men were practicing golf swings on a driving range.

OVERDUE PAYMENT

Jim mailed a check for the late payment. Then he went across town and sent another check for the same amount. If either check was delayed, then the other would probably arrive quickly. He figured that it was unlikely that both checks, if mailed from separate places, would be delayed. And the creditor would have received the next payment early, so that Jim would not have to ask for a refund.

WRONG ORDER

He put the lower-number check into a mailbox near his house. Then he drove to the post office and mailed the other check there. Because the second check did not have to wait for mailbox collection, Jim expected it to be delivered sooner than the first check.

I'VE GOT YOUR NUMBER

Kingfist found the telephone wiring that led into Sam's house and put one pin into each wire. Then he connected a telephone to the pins and dialed a long-distance number that was sure to answer, carefully charging the call on a telephone calling card. A few days later, he called his long-distance carrier and asked about possible misuse of the card and named the number that he had called. He easily learned the number that he had called from.

COLLECTING BACKWARDS

Not enough money was in the debtor's account for the check to clear. Kingfist merely found out how much money he needed to deposit for the check to be good, then deposited it and quickly cashed the check. This procedure reduced, although it did not eliminate, the debt.

BETTER LATE THAN PROMPT

Kingfist knew that the payments on the original contract were higher than the limit at the small claims court. He restructured the loan so that he could sue in small claims court every time a payment was missed. A small filing fee would induce major inconvenience for the debtor, who would have to repay the filing fee also. By restructuring the loan, Kingfist avoided all collection expenses which he could not recover. The debtor knew that major credit problems would exist from multiple unpaid judgments and scrupulously repaid the debt.

THE DEBTOR PAID

He went to small claims court, got a judgment, and sold the loan, with its judgment, to a racist extremist group of an ethnic background different from that of the customer. The extremist group was happy to receive the right to harass legally someone of its least-favored race, exceeded the limits of the law in its enthusiasm, and scared the debtor into paying. Laws that restrict collection agents, those who are hired to collect money on behalf of someone else, do not apply to creditors directly. Selling a judgment at a heavy discount can therefore be a prudent business practice, for it bypasses the collection-agent restrictions and may scare other debtors into paying promptly.

SHE WAS IN THE HOSPITAL

She was a recently hired trauma surgeon and was working in the operating room.

APPENDICITIS

Since the earlier surgery, Zeke had remarried.

CROSSED VISION

If you cross your fingers, then there will be creases at the joints that will allow a small amount of light to pass between your crossed fingers. By looking at objects through the gaps between your fingers, you will expose your eye to only those rays of light that went through one small space. By doing so, you will see a sharply focused image even without wearing eyeglasses. This fact is unimportant except to people who need strong eyeglasses, but who are not wearing them at a particular time.

Night Blindness Cure

1. Do you get night blindness only when driving your car?
2. When did you last clean and aim your headlights?

A Sweet Problem

Diabetic ulcers. According to alternative-medicine practitioners, sugar is a good medicine to apply to skin ulcers, blisters, and other open sores.

Miracle Cures

After pretending to have a serious back injury and collecting a large judgment, a malingering patient can go to a well-known source of miracle cures and pronounce himself recovered without leaving any evidence of fraud.

Not a Trusted Doctor

Cassandra, unknown to her recently met boyfriend, had completed medical school and was a licensed physician. She carefully hid her income-earning ability from men whom she did not know well because she did not want to be exploited. She was as much a doctor as was any other medical school graduate and was telling the truth. She considered the senility treatment worthless, and she said so.

The Plumber's Pressure

He had arteriosclerosis, which made his arteries more rigid than those of most people. Measuring blood pressure by compressing an artery and listening is unreliable if the artery is inflexible. The plumber recalled his use of pressure gauges while at work and the ineffectiveness of measuring water pressure in steel pipes by merely pinching them, and he very sensibly wondered if his blood pressure was really high.

Rx Lead Poisoning

Chelation with EDTA is the recommended treatment for lead poisoning, and most insurance companies pay for that treatment. It is also, according to many doctors, a useful treatment for atherosclerosis; but most insurance companies don't pay for it for that diagnosis. The doctor was unwilling to falsify a laboratory test, but craftily noted that the patient could be maneuvered into receiving appropriate treatment that would be insured without the necessity for making any false statements whatever.

Long Walk for the Disabled

He injured his neck and could no longer turn his head far enough to drive backwards easily. Therefore, he favored parking spaces that he could enter and leave without driving backwards, even if they were a long walk from his destination. To warn away children when he was forced to drive backwards, he installed a warning-tone device on his back bumper and wired it to his back-up lights.

Happy with the TV Ad

The man was a political candidate running for a local office. Tipped off that his rival had bought a 30-minute infomercial time slot, he bought the minute just before it and broadcast a test pattern, hoping to induce television viewers not to continue watching that particular channel.

Time for Repairs

When he first looked at his watch in the morning, it showed the time 10:01. Later that morning, it showed 11:11. During his lunch break, it showed 12:21. The rest of the morning, it did not show the correct time. Dilton was unknowingly wearing his digital watch upside down.

Strange Sounds

Some movies in the 1980s had scenes in which someone was typing, but the sounds of the keys were unrelated to the motion of the typist's fingers. Nowadays, scenes of typing conceal the hands to prevent that error. Reverberations remain a clue, as when a person walks from the outdoors into a narrow corridor and the footsteps do not reverberate indoors. Another clue is the absence of a companion sound, as when several people are walking and only one set of footsteps is heard. Or when a horse-drawn cart is shown and horses' hoofs are heard—but the cartwheels themselves are totally silent.

Watching the Game

Satellite signals are generally scrambled. To receive them in usable form, you buy an electronic device (a transponder) and pay royalties to the satellite company, which in turn sets your transponder to unscramble the appropriate signals. Elmer's accomplice ran a sports bar in a distant city and also had a transponder. To obtain unscrambled signals of locally blacked-out games, they merely swapped transponders.

Digital Downfall

Non-digital media merely record the sound waves as heard. Sound waves consist of fluctuations in air pressure, and a microphone can translate those fluctuations to fluctuations in an electrical signal that is in turn stored on magnetic tape or on a vinyl disk. Digital recording, however, translates the fluctuations to signals that represent the amplitudes and frequencies of the various components of the sound. But those signals don't match the timing of the wave cycles properly, so that the different pure tones that constitute a composite sound may be recorded out of phase and sound different when played back than when first recorded. Partially for that reason, they don't properly record overtones, which are high-frequency sounds that result from two or more lower-frequency sounds in harmony.

The TV Obeyed

Eager to show off his elaborate new equipment, Jake had friends over. Not only did he set up his videocassette player, but also he carefully reviewed the instructions for his television set, which included a timer that would turn it off a specified time later. He carefully set the shutoff timer to outlast the movie by a minute or two and, when the ad came on, saw a warning on the screen that the television would turn itself off in a couple of seconds. He knew that it would be shutting off immediately, so he shouted at the television set just for the fun of it.

The VCR Timers

Jenny noted that the device was battery-powered and could be programmed to tell the VCR to record Benny's favorite show every night. But if the VCR wasn't plugged in, then it wouldn't record anything. Therefore, Jenny got two 24-hour timers and set them each to be on for 12 hours. She plugged one timer into the wall, the other timer into the first timer, and the VCR into the second timer. Because the first timer delivered power only 12 hours out of 24, the second timer would do a complete cycle in 48 hours. It would deliver power to the VCR during 12 of those 48 hours, and Jenny set the timers so that the 12-hour periods included the time of Benny's show during alternate nights. It was easy to plug the VCR temporarily into an ordinary outlet when playing tapes or for other purposes.

THE VCR REMOTE CONTROL

Except for the nuisance of long cables and a small loss of signal, there is no reason for a videocassette recorder to be close to a television set. Jenny merely moved the VCR to a shelf built into their headboard, where they could both easily reach it while in bed, and connected it to the TV with a long cable.

NO TELEVISION TROUBLE

A pocket-size television set was on top of the dashboard, and it was off. Stuart was listening to an audiocassette with his favorite show's theme music.

INEFFICIENCY PAYS OFF

An air conditioner. The models with the most cooling power have stronger motors and cost more than those with less power. But because they cool air substantially, only a small fraction of the air in a room needs to pass through the mechanism to cool a room by a specified amount. Most of the air in the room does not pass through the air conditioner as the room gets cool. What does pass through it is sufficiently cold to cool the entire room. But as temperature goes down, relative humidity goes up. The dissolved moisture in most of the air is not removed, and a too-strong air conditioner makes a room feel not only cool but also damp.

WORTH TWENTY DOLLARS

Any Federal Reserve bank would have exchanged the $20 bill, but would have insisted that ordinary currency is legal tender in payment of debts and replaced it with another $20 bill. Unless the original bill was damaged by fire or otherwise hard to spend, there is little reason to make such an exchange.

SLOW-WITTED CUSTOMERS

The menus of the fast-food restaurants offer soft drinks in different-sized cups, labeled "Small," "Medium," and "Large," with correspondingly different prices. Then the restaurants also offer unlimited free refills on the same soft drinks!

BANKING ON THE BOYCOTT

As the first man suggested, a group agreed to place special orders and overwhelm the help. The second man's strategy involved unusual denominations of money. The first people to place special orders were equipped with fifty- and hundred-dollar bills to force the cash registers to run out of small denominations. By taking a bite out of food before offering to pay for it, the group members would force acceptance of their large bills. The next people in the group got Susan B. Anthony dollars, which are easily confused with quarters, and half dollars and two-dollar bills. These unfamiliar but legal denominations would not fit easily into cash registers and would confuse the cashiers, who would be out of ordinary denominations. Properly done, with angry customers demanding their change, this maneuver would force the chain to generate ill will and lose money.

OLD MONEY BUT GOOD MONEY

United States currency formerly included silver certificates, which stopped being redeemable for silver in 1968. Since then, there has been no formal precious metal backing to guarantee its value. The year 1968 was also the first year that denominations higher than one dollar suggested the fear of currency devaluations by carrying the words "In God We Trust." Religious zealots favored the wording; some conservative economists took warning.

Secret Business

The men were planning a big business deal, and they were pretty sure that their telephones were tapped. They used a simple scrambler that could easily be obtained by an eavesdropper. But before the telephone conversation, they wrote a script for a fake conversation in which they discussed doing the opposite of what they really planned to do. They wanted eavesdroppers to anticipate the wrong plans and lose money, which the two men would gain. A secure scrambler would not have allowed eavesdroppers to hear the staged conversation and would not have helped the two men.

Gas-Station Glitch

The man whom George paid was not an employee of the station, but a con artist who got a uniform, asked everyone in line for ten dollars, and left quickly.

Marketing Muddle

The Kia is marketed with the crossbar of the Λ missing: KIΛ. The Λ is the Greek-alphabet equivalent of our letter L, which means that USA customers who know the Greek alphabet may read K-I-L and wonder about the auto's safety.

Easy Money

Butch stole the television sets from his employer, making a profit of $30 for each set that he sold.

Too Much Money

The investor was going to be a limited partner. Someone who invests in a company as a limited partner does not have the right to manage the company, not even partial or voting rights. Such an arrangement is common and completely legal and ethical. Without management authority, the investor wouldn't be concerned about losing control to other investors. What worried him were the personal finances of the people who were going to manage the company. They could have invested all of their money in it, but didn't. If they had a lot of money outside the company, then the investor feared that they expected the company to fail.

LOTTERY LOGIC

Lottery tickets or other risky investments are very sensible when bankruptcy is imminent. Suppose, for example, you have $10,000 in assets and $20,000 in liabilities. If you merely pay your debts to the best of your ability, then you are certain to go broke. But if you buy as many lottery tickets as you can afford, then you have a chance of winning more than what you owe. Then you would be able to pay your debts and have some money left over. Although winning a large amount of money is unlikely, it is possible. That possibility converts certain bankruptcy into a chance to be rich.

YOUTHFUL GAMBLE

College students, despite uniform room charges, are often assigned dormitory rooms of unequal sizes by lottery. Similarly, equal tuition payments do not necessarily result in equal education, because lotteries are used to select which students get access to popular courses that have enrollment quotas.

STAGED ROULETTE

The police chief had a crooked gambling joint raided and easily obtained a rigged roulette wheel for the show.

THE DEADLY SCULPTURE

He lived in a tower on a hill. Being poor, he had no money for materials, so he took the copper lightning rod from the building. He made a beautiful statue with the copper, but soon afterward the tower was struck by lightning and he was killed.

Peak Performance

In the climber's knapsack was his national flag, which he would have planted on the summit had he reached it.

The Fatal Fish

The man's boat had capsized and he was adrift in an inflatable dinghy in a cold ocean. He caught a fish and, while cutting it up, his knife slipped and punctured the dinghy.

Adam Had None

The letter e.

Shot Dead

The woman was a Russian sniper who, during the siege of Stalingrad in World War II, shot several German soldiers.

Would You Believe It?

The second person was underwater, so the block floated up. The third person was on a space station, where there was no gravity, so when the block was released it floated unsupported.

Jailbreak

The man knew that his escape would be detected after about half an hour. He escaped at 10:30 on Tuesday morning just 30 minutes before the routine weekly alarm test, when everyone in the surrounding area would ignore the siren.

Sitting Ducks

The woman is an aeronautics engineer. She uses the gun to shoots ducks at airplane engines to test how they handle high-speed impacts with birds.

Bald Facts

After Mary, Queen of Scots had been beheaded, the executioner held up her head to show it to the mob. The head fell out of the wig.

Lethal Action

The Brazilian customs authorities require that all imported fruit be sprayed with pesticides to prevent insects or diseases from reaching domestic crops. They sprayed the hold of a fruit ship arriving from the Ivory Coast in Africa just before it docked in Brazil. They subsequently found the bodies of 10 stowaways who had hidden in the ship's hold and who had been poisoned by the pesticides.

Recognition

His Aunt Mary and his mother were identical twins.

Destruction

The body of a very overweight man is being cremated. There is so much fat that the crematorium catches fire and is burned down.

Wonderful Walk

During his walk in the woods, the man picked up several burrs on his clothes. When he returned home, he examined them under his microscope and discovered the mechanism whereby they stick on. He went on to invent Velcro.

Pesky Escalator

The foreign visitor saw a sign saying, "Dogs must be carried." He did not have a dog!

Poles Apart

Before the expedition the explorers deliberately ate a lot of fatty foods and put on several pounds of extra weight so that the fat would serve as food and fuel.

Arrested Development

The bank robber dashed to the revolving door and tried to push it in the direction in which it would not revolve.

Holed Out

The golfer's ball rebounded off the head of another golfer who was crossing the green. The ball bounced into the hole. However, the man who was hit died.

Trunk-ated

A policeman suspects that there is the body of a murdered man in the trunk. He dials the cell phone of the victim and the phone is heard ringing in the trunk.

Sports Mad

The man wanted to record his favorite football team on TV. However, the safety tab on his only videocassette had been removed and he needed to cover the space with tape.

Appendectomy I

The patient was a man who was going on a polar expedition in the first years of the 20th century. If he got appendicitis in such a remote region, he would die due to lack of treatment, so his healthy appendix was removed as a precaution.

Appendectomy II

Shell shock was not recognized as a genuine medical condition during World War I. Sympathetic surgeons often removed perfectly healthy appendixes from shell-shock victims so they could be sent home on medical grounds.

Riotous Assembly

The institution was a university. Rioting students had raided the geology department and used rock samples as ammunition.

Kneed to Know

The wife of the deaf Thomas Edison used to go with him to the theater. She drummed out on his knee in Morse code with her fingers what the actors were saying on stage.

Bad Trip

The anti-drug agency distributed pencils that had TOO COOL TO DO DRUGS printed on them. As the children sharpened the pencils down, the message became—COOL TO DO DRUGS and eventually just DO DRUGS.

WALLY Test I Answers

1. Because it has more geese in it!
2. Because they all have telephone lines!
3. So that he can fit in the small spaceship.
4. Exactly where you left him!
5. One. It takes many bricks to build the house but only one brick to complete it.
6. Take away his credit cards!
7. Edam is "made" backward.
8. A mailman.
9. Wet.
10. Take away their chairs.

Rate your score on the following scale:

Number Correct	Rating
8 to 10	WALLY Whiz
6 to 7	Smart Aleck
3 to 5	WALLY
0 to 2	Ultra-WALLY

Two Letters

The man is given the world's most difficult crossword and offered a prize of $100 for every letter he gets right. He puts "S" for each initial letter and "E" in every other space. S is the commonest initial letter and E the commonest letter in the English language.

Body of Evidence

The woman is a cleaner who wipes the fingerprints from a murder weapon in the course of her dusting.

Shakespeare's Blunder

The identical twins Viola and Sebastian are different sexes. This is impossible.

No Charge

The man was totally deaf, so he did not hear his rights being read to him by the arresting officer.

Pond Life

Because silk hats came into fashion, the demand for beaver hats decreased. More beavers meant more small lakes and bogs.

Shoe Shop Shuffle

One shop puts left shoes outside as samples; the other three shops put right shoes out. Display shoes are stolen, but the thieves have to form pairs, so more are taken from the store showing left shoes.

Caesar's Blunder

Since the tides in the Mediterranean are very weak, Julius Caesar did not beach his ships high enough when he landed on the shores of England. Many ships floated off on the next tide and were lost.

Slow Death

Aeschylus was killed when the tortoise was dropped on him from a height by an eagle who may have mistaken the bald head of Aeschylus for a rock on which to break the tortoise.

Driving Away

The rich woman was very nearsighted, but did not like wearing glasses or contact lenses. So she had her windshield ground to her prescription. The thief could not see clearly through it.

Lit Too Well?

During the blitz in World War II, London was subjected to heavy bombing by German planes. Sussex is south of London. It is on the flight path from Germany and part of its coastline resembles the Thames estuary. The authorities put lights in fields and in empty countryside to look like blacked-out London from the air. Some German aircrews were deceived and dropped their bombs in the wrong place.

Quick on the Draw

The man's wife had played a trick on him. She called him to watch the drawing on TV and he was unaware that he was watching a video of the previous week's draw. She had bought him a ticket for today's draw and chosen the previous week's winning numbers.

Scaled Down

The butcher had only one turkey left. The customer asked him its weight and he weighed it. The customer then asked if he had a slightly heavier one, so the butcher put the turkey away and then brought it out again. This time when he weighed it, he pressed down on the scale with his thumb in order to give it an exaggerated weight. The customer then said, "Fine—I'll take both!"

The Happy Woman

She was playing golf and hit an eagle—two under par and a very good score.

Vandal Scandal

The authorities arranged for some chips of marble from the same original quarry source as the Parthenon to be distributed around the site every day. Tourists thought that they had picked up a piece of the original columns and were satisfied.

THE DEADLY DRAWING

She entered the room and saw the chalk picture outline of a body on the floor. It was the site of a recent murder and the chalk marked the position of the body.

LEONARDO'S SECRET

Leonardo hid the secret designs by painting over them with beautiful oil paintings. He knew that no one would remove such masterpieces. But he did not know that modern x-ray techniques would allow art historians to see through the oil paintings and reveal his designs.

DOWN PERISCOPE

The submarine started at sea and then sailed into a canal system, where each lock dropped the water level by 30 feet.

THE LETTER LEFT OUT

The letter W is left out because it can always be written as UU— double U!

ARRESTED DEVELOPMENT—AGAIN

Bank employees noticed that the two men were Siamese twins. This reduced the number of suspects dramatically.

TITANIC PROPORTIONS

One of the reasons why so many perished on the Titanic was the shortage of lifeboats. Laws were passed to ensure that all ships had adequate lifeboats for all crew and passengers. One small ship took on so many lifeboats that it sank under their weight. (It must have been overloaded already!)

THE MOVER

The letter t.

DEATH OF A PLAYER

The man was a golfer who absentmindedly sucked on his tee between shots. The tee had picked up deadly weed killer used on the golf course, and the man died from poisoning.

HOT PICTURE

The woman commissioned a tattoo artist to produce a beautiful tattoo on her husband's back as a birthday present. The picture was fine, but the next day the unfortunate man was killed in a motorcycle accident. He was cremated.

GENUINE ARTICLE

The play was written by Brian Shakespeare, a contemporary dramatist. He vouched for its authenticity.

UNHEALTHY LIFESTYLE

The man was a heavy smoker. His smoke kept away mosquitoes and other insects. The woman died from an insect bite.

NEW WORLD RECORD

The woman's great-great-granddaughter gave birth, so the old woman became the only known great-great-great-grandmother alive. The family had six generations alive at the same time.

DEATH BY ROMANCE

The couple spent their honeymoon on a trip to the Arctic. They stayed in an igloo. The fire melted a hole in the roof and they died of exposure.

PENALTY

It was the women's World Cup and the match was played in a country with strict rules about female nudity or undressing in public.

GOLF CHALLENGE I

The woman's handicap was more than two shots greater than the man's.

GOLF CHALLENGE II

They were playing match play. The woman won more holes than the man.

GOLF CHALLENGE III

They were playing darts—highest score with three darts.

POOR INVESTMENT

The house was in a beautiful clifftop location. But within a few years, coastal erosion accelerated, and nothing could stop the house from eventually falling into the sea.

Give Us a Hand . . .

The man was a diver searching for pearls in giant clams. A previous diver had had his hand trapped in the clam, and as his oxygen ran out the poor man was forced to cut off his own hand.

Evil Intent

The man happened to put his door key in his mouth (because he was holding lots of other things in his hands). The key tasted of soap. He deduced correctly that his visitor had taken an impression of the key in a bar of soap in order to make a duplicate key so that he could be burgled.

Two Heads Are Better Than One!

They were Native Americans who saw a European riding a horse. It was the first time they had seen a horse.

Stone Me!

David slew Goliath with a stone from his sling and a major battle was averted.

Judge for Yourself

The defendant sent the judge a cheap box of cigars and included the plaintiff's name card in it!

Love Letters

She was a divorce lawyer drumming up business!

Strange Behavior

The man saw a tree lying across the road. He was in Africa and he knew that blocking the road with a tree was a favorite trick of armed bandits, who then waited for a car to stop at the tree so that they could ambush and rob the passengers. He guessed correctly that this was the case here, so he reversed quickly to avoid danger.

Tree Trouble

The foundation of the wall cut through the roots of the ancient tree and killed it.

The Burial Chamber

The man was building the burial chamber of an Egyptian pharaoh in ancient times. He built the real burial chamber deep inside a pyramid. He also built another burial chamber that was easier to find that he deliberately wrecked so that when any future graverobbers found it, they would think that earlier graverobbers had found the tomb and taken the treasure.

Miscarriage of Justice

The Italian was Pontius Pilate, who released Barabbas and condemned Jesus Christ to die by crucifixion at Easter time. Every year Easter is marked by the sale of millions of chocolate Easter eggs worldwide.

Offenses Down

The police officers filled in their reports and forms while sitting in marked police cars parked outside the homes of known criminals. Drug dealers, fences, and burglars found it very inhibiting and bad for business to have a marked police car outside their houses. So crime went down.

Police Chase

The getaway vehicle was a double-decker bus that went under a low bridge. The top deck of the bus was cut off and fell onto the pursuing police car. (This is a famous scene in a movie featuring James Bond, Agent 007.)

Café Society

The café owner installed pink lighting that highlighted all the teenagers' acne!

Hi, Jean!

The shop owner introduced an electric insect zapper to kill flies and other insects that might land on the food. However, when the flies were "zapped," they were propelled up to five feet, and often fell on the food.

The Empty Machine

Kids had poured water into molds the size of quarters. The molds were placed in the deep freeze and the resulting ice coins were used in the machine. They subsequently melted and dripped out of the machine leaving no trace.

Take a Fence

The man had made green paint by mixing yellow paint and blue paint. The blue paint was oil-based, but the yellow paint was water-based. Heavy rain had dissolved the yellow paint, leaving the fence decidedly blue.

1. Lemon-aid
2. A lid.
3. The lion.
4. His horse was called "yet."
5. Get someone else to break the shell.
6. Because he was dead.
7. They use rope.
8. If they lifted up that leg, they would fall over.
9. Wintertime.
10. It wooden go!

Rate your score on the following scale:

Number Correct	Rating
8 to 10	WALLY Whiz
6 to 7	Smart Aleck
3 to 5	WALLY
0 to 2	Ultra-WALLY

SEX DISCRIMINATION

It was found that the female lawyers wore underwire bras, which set off the very sensitive metal detectors.

WEIGHT LOSS

The doctor running the clinic had noticed that people living at high altitudes were generally thin. The air is thinner and people use more energy in all activities, including breathing. He therefore located his diet clinic at 8,000 feet above sea level and the patients found that they lost weight.

PSYCHIC

You notice that the woman is carrying a kettle. It is a very cold morning and only one of the cars has the windshield de-iced. You deduce correctly that she has defrosted her windshield with the kettle and is returning it to her home before setting off on her journey.

THE HAPPY ROBBER

The man was robbing a blood bank. He stole some rare blood that his sick daughter needed for a life-saving operation. He could not have afforded to buy the blood.

SIEGE MENTALITY

Several of the attacking soldiers had died of the plague. Their bodies were catapulted over the walls, and they infected many of the defenders, who were in a much more confined space. The defenders soon surrendered.

CARRIER BAGS

It was seriously proposed that the British Navy tow icebergs from the north and shape the tops to serve as aircraft carriers. They could not be sunk, lasted quite a long time, and could be cheaply replaced. However, it was too lateral a solution for the Navy high command!

THE CATHEDRAL UNTOUCHED

On a moonlit night, the dome of St. Paul's cathedral acted like a shining beacon to guide German planes during the blackout, so they deliberately avoided bombing it.

BAGS AWAY

The passenger's pet dog escaped from his suitcase in the hold and bit through some of the plane's electric cables, thereby disrupting the plane's controls.

THE SAD SAMARITAN

Jim found the full gas can in the trunk of his car. He had driven off and left the motorist stranded.

THE TALLEST TREE

The men chopped down the tree and then measured it on the ground!

THE UNWELCOME GUEST

The couple gave the neighbor a good meal, and when he finished, they gave his scrap-filled plate to the dog, who proceeded to lick it clean. They then put the plate straight back into the cupboard—pretending that was their normal procedure. The neighbor did not come back for any more meals!

POOR SHOW

His name was Dick Fosbury, inventor of the famous Fosbury flop, a new high-jumping technique that involved going over the bar backward and that revolutionized the sport. He won the gold medal in the Mexico City Olympics in 1968.

MESSAGE RECEIVED

Alexander the Great had the envoy's head shaved and then the message was tattooed on the envoy's head. Then he let the man's hair grow for a few weeks. When the envoy arrived, his head was shaved to reveal the message.

THE MIGHTY STONE

The peasant first suggested putting props around the boulder to stabilize it. Then a team of workers dug a big hole around and halfway under the boulder. When the hole was big enough, they pulled away the props and the boulder rolled into the hole where it was then covered with earth.

THE WORLD'S MOST EXPENSIVE CAR

The most expensive car was the moon buggy used by astronauts to explore the moon. It was left there. Although NASA would like to sell it, no one can retrieve it!

THE FATAL FALL

The woman was running in the Olympics in her national relay team. She dropped the baton and her team ended up losing. When she later returned to her country, the tyrannical despot who ran it was so displeased that he had her shot.

ELECTION SELECTION

The successful candidate changed his name to "None of the Above." His name appeared on the list below the other candidates (Davies, Garcia, and Jones). The voters in the deprived area resented all the established political parties and voted for None of the Above as a protest.

WELL TRAINED

The child was correct. It was a mail train!

RAZOR ATTACK

The woman forgot to plug in the razor!

THE OLD CROONER

The owners of shopping malls found that if they used Bing Crosby songs for the music in the public areas, then they had fewer undesirable youngsters hanging around and less crime was committed.

THE PARSON'S PUP

The vicar wears black suits and knows that light-colored dog hairs will show up on his suits, but that black ones will not be noticed.

GENEROSITY?

The man robbed a bank and was chased on foot by the public and the police. He threw away much of the cash he had acquired, which caused some chasers to stop to pick up the money and caused a rumpus that delayed the police and allowed the criminal to escape. The people who picked up the bills were forced to give them back or face prosecution.

WATCH THAT MAN!

A picture of the runner early in the race showed him wearing his watch on his right wrist. When he crossed the finishing line, it was on his left wrist. The judges investigated further and found that one man had run the first half of the race and his identical twin brother had run the second half. They had switched at a toilet on the route.

THE TRACKS OF MY TIRES

The woman was the only person in a wheelchair.

THE UPSET WOMAN

He was a mouse caught in a mousetrap.

BERTHA'S TRAVELS

Bertha is an elevator operator.

SICK LEAVE

Walter was a newborn baby.

TOP AT LAST

William's name was William Abbott, and the results were given in alphabetical order.

CRIMINAL ASSISTANCE

The police put up notices "Beware of Pickpockets." The pickpockets stood near a sign and noticed that when people saw it they immediately checked that their purses and wallets were safe. The pickpockets then knew where their victims carried their purses and wallets—which made them easier to steal.

IN THE MIDDLE OF THE NIGHT

He turns on the light.

HONORABLE INTENT

The six people had all received different organs from a donor who had died in an accident. They meet to honor his memory.

SHELL SHOCK

The pea isn't under any of the shells. It's slipped under a shell by the operator as he lifts it. Sometimes the operator places the pea under a player's choice to encourage dupes.

WONDERFUL WEATHER

The ship was the Titanic, which hit an iceberg on a fine night when the sea was very flat. If the weather had been worse, then the lookouts would have seen waves hitting the iceberg or heard the iceberg. (Icebergs make groaning noises when they move.) Unfortunately the iceberg wasn't seen and the rest is history.

MATERIAL WITNESS

They are on the window!

DENISE AND HARRY

Denise and Harry were hurricanes.

MECHANICAL ADVANTAGE

It was raining heavily and the man discovered a leak in the roof of his car. He bought several packs of chewing gum, chewed them, and then used the gum as a waterproof filler until he could reach a garage.

LIFESAVER

The politician was Teddy Roosevelt, the American president. In 1912, in Milwaukee, he was shot in the chest. He was saved because the bullet was slowed as it passed through the folded manuscript of the speech in his breast pocket. He went on to make the speech later on the same day that he was shot!

UNFINISHED BUSINESS

His autobiography.

THE DEADLY DRESSER

The last thing he put on was his shoe and it contained a deadly spider that bit him, and he died soon after.

LANDLUBBER

He sailed around the coast of Antarctica.

ANOTHER LANDLUBBER

He was an astronaut in a space ship.

PLANE AND SIMPLE

The boy will be six inches taller than the nail. The tree grows from the top, so the nail won't rise.

JERICHO

The man was building a house of cards.

SUPERIOR KNOWLEDGE

One of the toilet seats had been left up.

Half for Me and Half for You

Lucrezia Borgia put a deadly poison on one side of the blade of a knife. When she cut the apple, only one half was poisoned.

Rush Job

He used the tough tent cloth to make trousers for the miners. His name was Levi Strauss.

The Engraving

She received a used British postage stamp.

Who Did It?

One of the words that was not rude was spelled incorrectly (for example, "The headmaster is a horribul %$@*&@!"). The teacher gave a spelling test that included the word and the guilty child spelled it wrong again.

Lethal Relief

The food was dropped by parachute in remote areas. Several people were killed when the packages fell on them.

Hot Job

The man wore a short-sleeved shirt and his name was tattooed on his arm.

Chop Chop

For a short time on sunny days, the shadow of the old tree covered an instrument used for recording sunshine. The instrument had been put in place on a cloudy day. Good sense prevailed and the instrument was moved instead.

Resistance

Pictures in buildings that would be occupied were hung at a slight angle and attached to bombs. The tidy Germans straightened the pictures with fatal results.

Basket Case

She was "Madame Guillotine," the deadly invention of Joseph Guillotin that was used in France to execute people.

Invisible Earnings

Nauru exports guano, which is an excellent fertilizer. Guano comes from the droppings of seabirds.

Absolute Madness

A bus driver was told to bring 20 psychiatric patients to a mental hospital. On the way he stopped to buy a newspaper. When he got back, all his passengers had gone. So he drove up to several bus stops and collected the first 20 passengers he could find and delivered them to hospital, where he warned the staff that they would all cause trouble and claim to be sane.

WALLY Test III Answers

Here are the answers to the first WALLY Test. Be prepared to groan!

1. No. He will take his glass eye out of its socket and bite it.
2. No. He will take out his false teeth and bite his good eye with them.
3. You stand back to back.
4. The shadow of a horse.
5. Mr. Bigger's son. No matter how big Mr. Bigger is, his son is a little Bigger!
6. Tom's mother's third child was named Tom.
7. Egypt, Greenland, and Niagara Falls.
8. A glove.
9. An amoeba.
10. A blackboard.

Rate your score on the following scale:

Number Correct	Rating
8 to 10	WALLY Whiz
6 to 7	Smart Aleck
3 to 5	WALLY
0 to 2	Ultra-WALLY

Spies Are Us

The German spies wore identical hats with secret information hidden inside the hatband. They entered the restaurant at slightly different times and placed their hats on the hatrack where they could see them. They left at different times—each taking the other's hat.

Tittle Tattle

A tittle is the dot on an i.

OUTSTANDING

The Old Farmer's Almanac had a hole in the top left corner that made it ideal for hanging on a nail in the outhouse.

THE STUFFED CLOUD

A stuffed cloud, in pilot slang, is a cloud with a mountain in it. The meteorologist was a passenger on a plane that hit a stuffed cloud. He was killed and had to be replaced at his job.

A STRANGE COLLECTION

The guests are eating pheasant, which they shot earlier that day. The container is for the pellets of lead shot.

FOREIGN CURE

The man is an alcoholic. He flies to a country where alcohol is banned by law in the hope of curing his addiction by removing the temptation.

BUS LANE BONUS

Emergency vehicles and, in particular, ambulances were allowed to use the bus lanes. Ambulances reached accident victims sooner and got them to the hospital sooner so fewer of them died.

BLOW BY BLOW

The assistant at the fairground blew darts through a concealed blowpipe to burst the balloons of children on their way home from the fair so that their parents would have to return to buy replacement balloons in order to stem the tears.

History Question

Absolutely nothing happened in London on September 8, 1752. It was one of the eleven days dropped when the old calendar was adjusted to the new one.

Sign Here

He bought two identical signs for his café, but found that he needed two different ones for the two sets of traffic coming in different directions. The two signs said:
"FRED'S CAFÉ fi" and "< FRED'S CAFÉ"

Paper Tiger

It's January and he is writing the date of the year on all the checks in his checkbook to avoid putting last year's date by mistake.

Forging Ahead

The forger bought a cheap item with the genuine $50 bill. In the change he would usually get at least one $20 bill. He would then ask the storekeeper to change the $20 bill into two tens and switch the genuine $20 bill with a forged one of his own making. The storekeeper was less likely to check a bill he believed he had just paid out.

Smile Please!

The man suggested that they make the hole in the top of the tube bigger so that more toothpaste would be squeezed out each time.

High on a Hill

The man was marooned on a volcano that had recently erupted. He was kept alive by the heat of the melting lava.

MINE SHAFTED

He had shredded real silver dollars to produce the silver. One piece was found with the word "unum" (from "e pluribus unum") on it.

THAT WILL TEACH YOU

The man left his glasses on his bedside table. They had focused the rays of the sun onto his pillow and started a fire that destroyed his house.

A GEOGRAPHY QUESTION

Hawaii is the most southern and Alaska is simultaneously the most western, most northern, and most eastern. It's the most eastern because some remote islands that are part of Alaska lie over the 180-degree line of longitude and are therefore east of the continental U.S.

THE GENEROUS GENERAL

The soldier thanked him by saying, "Danke schön."

FAST MOVER!

The man was a diplomatic courier and he visited the embassies of 30 countries, all situated in Washington. In law, an embassy is part of the country of the embassy and not part of the country in which it is situated.

RUNNING ON EMPTY

Mr. and Mrs. Jones had had a silly argument. Mrs. Jones stormed out and the depressive Mr. Jones had tried to commit suicide by sitting in his car in the garage with the engine running. He passed out, but then the car ran out of gas and when Mrs. Jones returned she rescued him and they were reconciled.

What's the Point?

The woman is a carpenter who works on scaffolding at a building site. A conventional round pencil is more likely to roll off and fall.

The Office Job

This happened in the 1800s. The man had applied for a job as a telegraph operator. Among the background noise was a Morse code message saying, "If you understand this, walk into the office." It was a test of the candidates' skill and alertness. He was the only candidate who passed.

Hearty Appetite

After the Exxon Valdez oil spill, an enormous amount of money was spent cleansing the environment and rehabilitating oil-damaged animals. Two seals had been carefully nurtured back to good health at a cost of over $100,000, and they were released into the sea in front of an appreciative crowd. A few minutes later the crowd was horrified to see them both eaten by a killer whale.

The Upset Bird Watcher

The ornithologist was sitting on a plane coming in to land when he saw the rare bird, which was sucked into the jet engine causing the engine to fail and the plane to crash-land.

Floating Home

The man was an astronaut.

Co-lateral Damage

They strengthened the parts of the aircraft that had not been hit.

Antiaircraft fire is random in nature. The returning planes showed damage that had not been fatal. But this sample excludes information from the planes that had not returned and had sustained fatal damage. It was deduced that they had sustained damage on the parts not hit on the returning planes. By adding armor to the planes, overall losses were reduced.

ORSON CART

Orson Welles's voice was recognized by the many children who listened to his regular children's radio show.

THROWING HIS WEIGHT ABOUT

He was demonstrating how strong the glass was to a group of visitors. He threw himself against it, but it was not as strong as he had thought.

DISCONNECTED?

The horse worked in a mill. It walked around in a circle all day to drive the millstone. In the course of the day, its outer legs walked a mile farther than its inner legs.

JOKER

When one player went to play a card, she knocked over a mug. The hot drink poured over the other player, who immediately jumped up and started to take her clothes off.

RICH MAN, POOR MAN

Rich people had bone china that could take the hot tea, but poor people had cheap crockery that would crack if hot tea were poured into it. Pouring the tea first became a sign of prosperity.

MINED OVER MATTER

The sailor used the water hose on the ship to direct a jet of water onto the mine to push it out of the path of the ship.

SURPRISE VISIT

The manager and staff dumped all the trash on the flat roof of the factory so that it wouldn't be seen. Unfortunately, the company chairman arrived by helicopter and landed on the roof.

SCHOOL'S OUT

She has just celebrated her 105th birthday, but the computer at the local education authority cannot recognize a date of birth that is over 100 years ago. Calculating that she is 5 years old, the computer prints out an automatic instruction to attend school.

THE DEADLY STONE

The man was lost in the desert. Without landmarks, he marked stones with a drop of blood from a cut on his hand. After two days of walking and out of water, he found a stone with blood on it. He knew that he was walking in circles and he shot himself rather than face a slower death.

THE COSTLY WAVE

The man was the winner of the prestigious London Marathon race. He waved to the large crowd the entire way down the finishing straightaway and, because of that, he just failed to break the record time for the marathon—thereby missing out on the $30,000 bonus prize.

WALLY TEST IV ANSWERS

More answers, more groans!
1. Snow.
2. Hide their shovels!
3. It was just a stage he was going through!
4. He was given the Nobel Prize.
5. Mickey Mouse.
6. He changed his name to Exit.
7. At a boxing arena.
8. A hare piece.
9. Don't feed him.
10. To get his feet in (all pants have three large holes).

Rate your score on the following scale:

Number Correct	Rating
8 to 10	WALLY Whiz
6 to 7	Smart Aleck
3 to 5	WALLY
0 to 2	Ultra-WALLY

2020 VISION

As he talked to the farmer on the phone, the newspaper editor realized that the man had a slight lisp and that what he had actually reported stolen was "two sows and twenty pigs."

THE DEADLY OMELET

The man was an aristocrat on the run from the French Revolution. He disguised himself as a peasant. When he ordered an omelet, he was asked how many eggs he wanted in it. He replied, "A dozen." No peasant would have asked for more than two or three.

THE GAP

The man was carving a tombstone. A husband had died and the man carved
PRAY FOR
HI M.
When the wife died, she would be buried with her husband and the engraving would be amended to
PRAY FOR
THEM.

THE DINNER CLUE

The meal included a large piece of stale cheese that the suspect bit into and then left. His teeth marks were found to match a bite on the body of a murder victim.

WRONG WAY

The bus from Alewife to Zebedee is always full by the time it reaches the man's stop, so he catches one going the opposite way in order to get a seat on the bus for the return journey to Zebedee.

THE SINGLE WORD

The word was "Guilty." I was foreman of the jury at the woman's trial.

The Man Who Would Not Read

He saw a notice on the side of the carriage that said, "This carriage is not for Reading." Reading is a town on the main line between London and Bristol.

Not Eating?

His plate is his dental plate.

Two Pigs

This happened in France. One pig was sold for bacon. The other had been painstakingly trained to sniff out truffles and was therefore very valuable.

Eensy Weensy Spider Farm

Spiderwebs are bought by unscrupulous wine merchants who want to give the impression that their wines are old and mature.

Face-off

The French tested their artillery by firing some shots into the mountains. This caused avalanches that killed many soldiers on both sides.

Cheap and Cheerful

The food is salmon. Previously he had choked on a bone in fresh salmon. The salt in canned salmon dissolves the bones and removes this danger.

UP IN SMOKE

In this true story, the cigars were insured under the man's general household policy as named items. He claimed against his insurance company on the grounds that the cigars had been destroyed in a series of small fires. The insurance company rejected the claim, pointing out that he had started the fires in order to smoke the cigars. He took the insurance company to court and won the case. The judge ruled that the insurance policy covered against loss by fire and that this was what had happened. The man was awarded $10,000. However, as he left the court he was arrested by the police on a charge of arson, based on his sworn testimony. He was found guilty and given a one-year suspended prison sentence.

SILLY CONE

Drinking cups in the shapes of cones were provided at water fountains. Since they couldn't be put down, people had to quickly drink the water. This sped up their breaks.

NOT THE FÜHRER

When the shoes were removed from the body, the man was found to be wearing darned socks. The soldiers did not believe that the Führer of the Third Reich would wear darned socks.

VASE AND MEANS

Bone china was discovered when an unfortunate worker fell into the kiln and became part of the product. Animal bones are used nowadays.

MY CONDIMENTS TO THE CHEF

Drug addicts were using his café and dipping their needles into his vinegar bottles because heroin is soluble in vinegar. He replaced the vinegar bottles with small packets of vinegar in order to stop the addicts from dipping their syringes into the bottles.

THE MAN WHO DID NOT FLY

In this true case, many vacationers who flew with a certain airline had their homes burglarized while they were away. The police added a false name (but real address) to the list and caught the burglar red-handed when he broke in. It turned out that his sister worked for the airline and passed the list of passenger addresses to her nefarious brother.

INHERITANCE

The younger son took his sword and cut off his hand before hurling it ashore. Since he had touched the shore before his brother, he was able to claim his father's kingdom. (This story is told of the kingdom of Ulster, and to this day a bloody red hand is used as the symbol of the province.)

STAMP DEARTH DEATH

The man was a terrorist letter-bomber. He sent a letter bomb, but didn't put enough stamps on it. It was returned to him and it exploded, killing him.

ROCK OF AGES

The man was listening to rock-and-roll music through his Walkman headphones in the kitchen. He had his hand on the kettle and his back to the door. When his wife came in, she saw him shaking violently but she heard no sound. She called to him but he didn't hear her. Thinking that he was suffering from an electric shock, she picked up a rolling pin and hit his arm, breaking it.

Quo Vadis?

The archaeologist was excavating a Roman quarry. The ruts in the road leading from the quarry were much deeper on the left than on the right. Since the carts leaving the quarry were much heavier than those returning, he deduced that the Romans drove on the left side of the road.

Pork Puzzler

The man was traveling to a strict Muslim country where alcohol was banned. He placed a small bottle of whiskey under a pack of bacon in his suitcase. He knew that if the customs officials at the airport of entry opened his suitcase they wouldn't touch the bacon and therefore his whiskey would be safe.

Frozen Assets

During World War II, the Russians built a railway line over the frozen Lake Ladoga in order to deliver supplies to the city of Leningrad, which was under siege from German forces. Its population was starving and there was no means of supply from the Russian side other than over the lake.

Turned Off

The man was Guglielmo Marconi, the pioneer of radio transmission. When he died in 1937, all the radio stations in the world observed a minute of silence as a mark of respect.

The Last Mail

Both letters were the same weight, a fraction under the weight at which a surcharge was charged. He put the correct postage amount in stamps on each letter. One had a single stamp of the correct value and the other had several stamps adding up to the correct value. When the letters were weighed, the one with the more stamps was over the limit and so more stamps were needed.

SMALL IS NOT BEAUTIFUL

Small cars were banned in Sweden because of the high incidence of accidents involving collisions with moose. Occupants of small cars suffered serious injuries, but large cars offered more protection.

THE DEADLY FEATHER

The man was a circus sword swallower. In the middle of his act someone tickled him with the feather and he gagged.

THE SEALED ROOM

He died from carbon dioxide poisoning, which takes effect before oxygen starvation.

WRITTEN DOWN

She is writing along the top of a closed book—on the top of the pages. Any letter with a horizontal line in it is difficult, since the pen tends to slip down between the pages.

PUBLICITY PUZZLER

The man has feet of different sizes—his left foot is 12 and his right foot is 13. He advertises to find a man with the opposite—a left foot size 13 and right foot size 12. Together they go shopping to find a shoe style that suits them both. They then buy two pairs, one 12 and one 13, before swapping shoes.

WHO WANTS IT ANYWAY?

A lawsuit.

KNIGHTS OF OLD

When knights in full armor rode past the king, they would raise the visor on their helmet so that the king could see them. This action in turn became the salute that military personnel give to higher officers.

SHAVE THAT PIG!

In China, live pigs were used like hot-water bottles to keep people warm in bed on cold nights. For the sleepers' comfort, the pigs were shaved first.

WATCH OUT!

The man is Count Dracula, who leaves his house for his nightly drink of blood. However, his watch has stopped and what he thinks is night is actually a solar eclipse. He is caught in the sunlight and dies.

THE WEDDING PRESENT

The man selected a beautiful crystal vase in a gift shop, but he knocked it over and broke it. He had to pay for it, so he instructed the shop to wrap it and send it anyway. He assumed that people would think that it had been broken in transit. Unfortunately for him, the shop assistant carefully wrapped every broken piece before sending the package.

MURDER MYSTERY

The man and woman lie badly injured after a car accident. The wife knows that they are both going to die and she fears that she will die first. They recently married and have no children from this marriage but each has children from a previous marriage. If she dies first, then all of the joint estate will go to his children. She kills her husband so that her children will inherit the entire estate.

INDEX

Page key: puzzle, *clues,* **answer**